**Feel Inspired.
Embark on *Your* Journey**

MOUNTAIN
Dream

WEI SAN TANG

Copyright © 2020 by Wei San Tang

Mountain Dream

All rights reserved. No part of this publication may be reproduced, distributed or transmitted in any form or by any means, including photocopying, recording, or other electronic or mechanical methods, without the prior written permission of the publisher, except in the case of brief quotations embodied in critical reviews and certain other noncommercial uses permitted by copyright law.

Although the author and publisher have made every effort to ensure that the information in this book was correct at press time, the author and publisher do not assume and hereby disclaim any liability to any party for any loss, damage, or disruption caused by errors or omissions, whether such errors or omissions result from negligence, accident, or any other cause.

Adherence to all applicable laws and regulations, including international, federal, state and local governing professional licensing, business practises, advertising, and all other aspects of doing business in the US, Canada or any other jurisdiction is the sole responsibility of the reader and consumer.

Neither the author nor the publisher assumes any responsibility or liability whatsoever on behalf of the consumer or reader of this material. Any perceived slight of any individual or organisation is purely unintentional.

The resources in this book are provided for informational purposes only and should not be used to replace the specialised training and professional judgement of a health care or mental health care professional.

Neither the author nor the publisher can be held responsible for the use of the information provided within this book. Please always consult a trained professional before making any decision regarding treatment of yourself or others.

Some names and identifying details have been changed to protect the privacy of individuals.

ISBN: 978-0-6450207-0-0 (Paperback)

Cover Design by 100Covers.com
Interior Design by FormattedBooks.com

A GIFT FOR YOU
Just to say thanks for buying my book,
I would like to give you the photo pack of my adventure to
Everest Base Camp, which you will also read from the book.

TO RECEIVE YOUR FREE GIFT,
FOLLOW THE LINK BELOW:
https://ex-animo.org/mountaindreambook

For my dearest family members: Mum, Dad, and my two brothers.

Of course, no-one is born into a family by choice, so I realise that I've been very blessed to grow up in such a wonderful family environment. Each of you has played a vital role in every growing experience I've had, positive and negative, and I know this will continue.

Thank you for always trusting me, having faith in me, and always choosing to stand by me.

*Dream lofty dreams, and as you dream, so you shall become.
Your vision is the promise of what you shall one day be;
your ideal is the prophecy of what you shall at last unveil.*

—James Allen

TABLE OF CONTENTS

INTRODUCTION XI

PART I 1
    1. All Because of My Father, the Great Mentor in My Life 3
    2. Blessings That Are Harder to See 15
    3. More Than Just Sight-Seeing 19
    4. Stepping Up to the New Environment 27
    5. The Adventure Attitude 37
    6. Let's Talk: Safe Self, Adventure Self 43
    7. A Heart of Giving 51
    8. Jumping Over the Fence of Fundraising 59
    9. The "Exercise Type" 67

PART II 75
    10. Nepal—Majesty and Mysticism 77
    11. Crisp Air, Close Calls 81
    12. Moving Beyond the Altitude Sickness Threshold 91
    13. Could This Be the End? 99
    14. Returning with a Heart of Gratitude 107
    15. Moments of Realisation 111
    16. The Final Test 117
    17. It's Not Over … Yet 123
    18. Conclusion—Sleeping Dreams, Wake Up! 129

ACKNOWLEDGMENTS 133
ABOUT THE AUTHOR 137
CAN YOU HELP? 139

INTRODUCTION—A NORMAL PERSON AND A DREAMER

Every great dream begins with a dreamer.
Always remember, you have within you the strength, the patience,
and the passion to reach for the stars to change the world.
—Harriet Tubman

My name is Wei San—and I had a wild dream. I said to myself, "One day, I want to trek to Everest Base Camp". And I did it.

Now, let's just stop here because there's something we need to clear up immediately: when you think of the people who go to Nepal to summit Everest or trek the trails around Everest—what kind of person do you envision? What are your assumptions?

Perhaps one of your assumptions is that's something only wealthy people can do. Not just because of travel and gear costs, simply because doing those excursions are so coveted and the number of places open is so few relative to the demand, that it is very expensive to buy a place on one of the excursions.

Perhaps you've also heard of how difficult and dangerous Everest-related excursions are, due to altitude and weather, and whatnot. This leads to another assumption: the people doing it aren't just wealthy, but also very fit. Strong, long-time, ambitious, hardcore fitness and outdoors people.

If you hold these assumptions around Everest trekkers, then you probably assume I must be someone with a lot of disposable income, lots of time to train and travel, and I must be a long-time fitness devotee. A gifted athlete who is a natural when it comes to most anything physical.

Let's meet the real Wei San, shall we? I grew up in a middle-class family in Malaysia. I'm the youngest and the only daughter in my family (I have two older brothers). As I stepped into my adult life, I entered into the full-time workforce, similar to most people. Activities that I involve myself in include playing the flute in a community band, volunteering, and I love to read books. Other than participating in the little kids swim team for a year in primary school—and not swimming so well!—I've not done any organised athletics in my life. I did start walking at my father's encouragement when I was a kid, and I started to take it more seriously when I was in my early 20s. You'll read about this. The income I make from my work is what I live on. As I want to travel and see other parts of the world too, I plan around what I am capable of.

Even with this normal background, in 2017, when the universe presented me with an opportunity to take part in a fundraising trek to Everest Base Camp, I chose to say, "Yes!" At that point, I didn't know how I'd be able to pull it off, in terms of training, money, time, and important factors like that. With a lot of help from a lot of people and a year of preparation, I did it. I trekked to Everest Base Camp.

I've written this book because I want others, like you, to see from my example the awesome power of deciding on a big dream and putting in the effort to pursue it. I have a longtime personal mission to spread positive energy in our world, and as I see it, when we break our mould of automated living and dare to decide on a dream and then take action to pursue it, we create positivity, vibrancy, and passion in ourselves that then spreads to others. We make others and the world a better place.

In this book, I present my journey of discovery. In this journey you'll read about an ordinary person—me—who is contending with ordinary obstacles. Like fear of leaving my comfort zone. Fear of failure. Fear of getting rejected by others. Fear that my own body will not be strong enough. Even with all these obstacles coming at me, I managed to decide on a dream—a dream that for so many reasons suggested I wasn't the type to achieve it—and by leveraging the trust that others have in me to make it happen, I took action. It took over a year of action for me to finally make it to Nepal. And then the trek itself required even more action, even more negative barriers and obstacles coming at me to contend with in order to achieve my goal.

An ordinary person who dares to live a vibrant life, who dares to dream and work through the many obstacles that ordinary people face to pursue their dreams—that's this story. The result: I am creating a life that is meaningful, satisfying, and one where I see possibility, for myself and others, all around me.

Surely, you are not different from me. Surely, if I am able to do it, dream big and achieve it, then so can you! I love to read and listen to incredible stories of ordinary people who turn their dream to reality. Those stories inspire me and give me the gift of courage to follow suit. Through this book, I hope to provide you with similar inspiration and boldness. I would like to help you to awake the sleeping dream inside yourself.

Let's spread positivity in our world, starting with ourselves. That means—embracing and espousing our own "Yes, I can!" attitude.

PART I.

LIFE EXPERIENCES—MY TEACHERS THAT TAKE ME CLOSER TO MY DREAMS

1.

ALL BECAUSE OF MY FATHER, THE GREAT MENTOR IN MY LIFE

All our dreams can come true, if we have the courage to pursue them.
—Walt Disney

It all began with my first successful summit of a mountain peak. For me, that was Mount Kinabalu in Sabah, Malaysia. At 4,095 metres, it is the highest peak in Borneo's Crocker Range, and it is also the highest peak in Malaysia, where I was born.

To be clear, trekking isn't an activity that I'm naturally drawn to. It's not something that I've always enjoyed. In fact, for much of my life, doing long walks, and particularly long walks uphill and downhill, I've not enjoyed at all. However, something I did correlate was doing a long trek and having a nice dinner out afterwards as a reward. Yes, I love great food! Sure, it might not be the best motivator, but at least in the beginning, when I started, it kept me at it long enough to actually grow an interest in trekking itself.

Over time, I've found many reasons that motivate me beyond the great food reward. First, is the satisfaction of completing each trek. The beginning is tough, but I know that when I keep going, one step at a time, I will get there. Also, when I stand at a peak, having a bird's eye view, savouring the moment, that motivates me. Finally, knowing that by putting in effort upfront, I will be able to enjoy the fruits when the time comes—that's a big motivator.

The whole reason I ever dared climb Mount Kinabalu was all because of my father. Let me backtrack a bit to explain. I come from a close family that resided in Johor Bahru in West (or Peninsular) Malaysia. For work, my father ended up moving to Sabah in East Malaysia. For those of you who don't know the geography of Malaysia, there are two major parts to the country, Peninsular Malaysia to the west and East Malaysia to the east. They are separated by the South China Sea. So, my father's work that moved him to Sabah in East Malaysia was a big deal. My mother decided to move with him, seeing as Sabah was far away and in a place where we didn't have family ties. As for me and my brothers, they were already adults and living on their own, but I was still in secondary school. I wanted to stay in Johor Bahru where I'd grown up and finish secondary and high school there though my parents would be in East Malaysia. And this is what I did. Upon graduating from high school, I ended up moving to Sabah to study at the University of Sabah in Kota Kinabalu. However, by that time, Dad had already retired, and both my parents were back in Johor Bahru. So as a university student I was in, what was for me, very new territory.

Of course, like we all do, I have wondered if I would've followed a better path if I hadn't chosen to go to Sabah for university. But, there's no point to these musings. No matter what, my decision to go to Sabah has shaped many great outcomes for my life. For example, towards the end of my first year in university, Dad suggested we attempt the climb to Mount Kinabalu summit. The adventurous side of me shouted a big and loud, "Yes!" And so, a first important life dream was born for me: summiting Mount Kinabalu.

After the decision, I started to plan my training. The university campus was big enough to serve as a good training ground. The school provided us with shuttle buses to move between lecture halls and student housing. The first thing that came to my mind—skip the shuttle bus and walk. My dormitory was at the top of a short hill. There was a long staircase to ascend every time I wanted to return to my dorm. Also, I had friends who stayed in the lower area of campus, so that made an even longer walk to visit them and return to my dorm. For about two months, I trained in this way, all the while studying for exams and eagerly anticipating the trek.

Once exams finished, Dad flew from Johor Bahru to Kota Kinabalu, the day before our adventure. Waking in the morning, the day Dad came to pick me up, with my luggage packed, I felt feverish. "Am I really ready for this?" I wondered. I talked myself out of my anxiety, "It's okay, we have a couple of days before we attempt the climb. Don't get disheartened, focus on resting before the big day".

In the end, I got over my anxiety and fear. While I may not have realised it at the time, there were some key things that helped me to not give up. I had a very strong desire to attempt the climb. It was a challenge, and I like challenges too. Also, I knew that by doing it, by summiting a peak like this, it would take me to the next level in terms of my fitness and the possibilities and goals I could make in regard to trekking. And, I would like to honour the level of confidence Dad had in me. He showed that when he made the suggestion in the first place. Last on the list, also a powerful one, was my excitement to attempt the climb with Dad. I knew it would be one of those father-and-daughter moments that we would remember forever.

The day we arrived at the Kinabalu Park Headquarters, the base of the mountain, we found out there were no vacancies at the Laban Rata Resthouse. A bit of background, elevated at 3,270 metres, Laban Rata is the place where climbers typically spend the night after ascending from the base and before ascending to the peak, which normally happens early in the morning. So, it's a place for resting before summiting. And because there is a daily limit to the number of permits issued for climbing, a sleeping space at Laban Rata is tied closely with that. No permit, no climb.

The reservation clerk told us we could be on the waiting list, as sometimes there were cancellations and the permit could be reissued to those on the waiting list. We took his suggestion. We thought we could make use of the waiting days to explore and do shorter treks before the big ascent. We felt optimistic about our chances of landing a sleeping space at the Laban Rata Resthouse. It wasn't the climbing season after all.

That day, we checked into our room at a lodge at the base and had an early rest. The next day, we had an early breakfast, followed by a walk. We were exploring the park when Dad's mobile rang. My hope came true: there was a cancellation and two sleeping spaces were available at Laban Rata. So we would be issued with the climb permits that day. It was about 10 am when we got this news. Without wasting much time, we headed straight back to rearrange our backpacks for the climb from the base where we were at, up to the resthouse. I was super excited and felt so blessed with our luck.

It was around noon when we started our climb at the Timpohon Gate (1,866 metres) up to Laban Rata (3,270 metres). What I remember of the walk was a lot of uphills. It was an ascent, so, of course, this makes sense! The start didn't feel easy, especially because we were starting later than the usual early-morning start time and both of us had already used up our early-morning energy. This meant the climb felt particularly difficult.

At some point, I experienced an internal conflict. One voice asked, "Why did you bring us here to go through this?" Then my other voice fought back, "Don't listen to her. Come on, don't give up! One step at a time. No-one said this was going to be easy. It takes courage to be here. You are courageous, Tang Wei San! Trust yourself! The reward awaiting is worth the effort. This is a challenge that we committed to, and let's do it—no matter how!"

I always admired Dad's wisdom. "Always be prepared and do whatever you can to remove any possible distractions"—one of the many pearls of wisdom I learnt from him. Something that gave me encouragement on this mountain-ascent trek, was that we'd already decided to hire a porter to carry our backpacks for us. The backpacks carried the essential things that we needed for the climb and for our stay at Laban Rata. So we were carrying very little weight, really just our drinking water. That made things easier.

With much determination, we reached the Laban Rata Resthouse at about 7 pm. The kitchen was closing by the time we arrived, and most of the other climbers were resting by that time. According to the itinerary, the summit the following day would start at 2.30 am. That was to allow enough time to reach the summit and witness the sunrise. Our guide and porter were thoughtful. They knew we were hungry and needed dinner, not only for that night but also to keep us going the next day. They spoke to the kitchen staff who offered to cook fried rice for us. Even asking if that would be alright for us.

"What? Of course, that's more than alright", I thought to myself in this heart-warming moment.

We finished our dinner quickly as we did not want to hold up the staff. Then with sincere thanks, we said good night to everyone. That night, I drifted into the land of sleep with a heart of gratitude, so thankful we were able to make it this far.

Early morning the next day, I woke up before the alarm went off because I was so eager to get started. I was feeling fresh and excited as well. While brushing my teeth, I was imagining how it would feel to be at the peak. Something I'd been envisioning since I'd decided to do this trek several months earlier.

It was pitch dark out when we started our journey. Although we had our headlamps, I could not see much, only what fell in the scope of the light. So I followed very closely behind our guide. Dad was behind me, and our porter was last. It was a steep ascending trail. We were expecting an increase of elevation of 800 metres to the summit. There were steps, many steps that we were walking up. I was sweating heavily, but I couldn't take off a layer as it was actually cold out, especially with the wind blowing. The steps also challenged my breathing because the air got thinner, the higher we climbed. I also remember there was a tricky part where we needed to make use of a rope to pull ourselves up a very steep section. This really stretched my body.

As we went higher, the vegetation reduced to bushes and eventually we were climbing across a bare granite rockface. There was a thick white rope that trailed all the way to the summit. At first, I wasn't sure what it was for, and I didn't have the extra capacity in my brain to process it. Later on, I came to know that the rope was to help climbers to not lose their way to the summit in the dark. What a brilliant idea, I thought. As I climbed the final section across the open rockface towards the summit, the surrounding skyline lit up with the sun slowly rising.

We reached the summit in time to witness one of the most majestic sunrises I've viewed in my life. The dark surrounding us slowly gave way to the yellow sun. As the sun lit up the entire mountain area, a breathtaking 360-degree view from the peak revealed itself. How different from standing at the peak of the small hill back in our hometown! I could clearly see the uniqueness of the rocky landscape that made up the many nearby peaks. At that moment, I felt like I was in the heavens with the morning fog covering some of the area before the sun touched it. Standing at the summit with Dad on that day was a special moment. It has been 16 years since we did the climb, and that moment still stands very clearly in my mind.

There was a sign at the summit for people to take photos with. You know, "we were here" kind of photos. We joined the short queue to get a photo with our amazing guide and porter. When it was our turn, I passed the camera to another climber who was happy to take the photo of us. As we were posing, the guy shouted, "The camera shut down by itself!" "Err …" I thought. It turned out that I'd forgotten to charge the battery the night before, and the battery had gone dead. So, we ended up at the summit with no photo. Even so, that in itself remains a firm memory.

We took the time to enjoy the peaceful moment at the peak without any photos, but not for long. As our bodies started to cool down from the trek up, I actually felt very cold. Dangerously so, as it was sub-zero temperatures at the summit. That's when we decided it was time to make our way down to Laban Rata.

Now, descending in the daytime, I could actually see the route we'd taken on our way up. Wow! It actually looked a bit scary—the downward trail with the same white rope that had guided us on our way up. "Did we go up on this same route?" I wondered. Although I had that doubt for a couple of seconds, apparently it was the same route. I had to shake away the thought of possibly missing a step and becoming a giant ball rolling down the rockface. That would not be fun. At all.

As it was just me and Dad, we took our time walking the descent, and this gave me a little bit of room to process our surroundings. With the rocky surface around the summit behind us, what slowly came into view as we descended was mountain vegetation and the many steps, almost like a grand staircase. At one point, I saw tiny villages far down below us. Only then did I grasp the reality of exactly how high up we were on the trail. Everything beneath looked so small, and yet we were even smaller in the eyes of Mother Nature.

As it is natural to want to move faster because it is easier walking downhill, I had to be careful to maintain my focus. I didn't want to move fast and end up slipping and injuring myself. The way I did it was remembering what my father always said as we trekked smaller hills together: never lose sight of the importance of finishing the trek safely. If we want to be able to do it again and again, then we have to learn to celebrate at the bottom, not just at the top. With that, I asked myself not to get overconfident just because I'd reached the top of the mountain. I reminded myself, "This is not the finish yet, not until I reach the base". As the descending puts a lot of pressure on the knees too, I made use of that to be careful, stay focused, and watch every step.

We made it back to the Timpohon Gate tired and yet satisfied. A great sense of achievement filled me. We'd aimed to reach the top in a safe way, we'd also aimed to reach the base in a safe way—and we did it! Dad also emphasised that this was not only applicable to climbing but also to many things in life.

For the next week or so, we both had sore legs. I remembered I was doing my best not to bend my knees when I went up or down stairs for that next week. And poor Dad who still had to drive us as we began a road trip right after our climbing adventure. It was a manual car that we had rented, so you can imagine the exertion it required from his tired and sore legs.

Second Time Around

Mount Kinabalu is the jewel of Sabah. It's Malaysia's highest peak and is famous for its beauty. The granite peaks are often surrounded by clouds, which adds a layer of mystery to its hidden face. Then on the rare clear day, the summit reveals itself: a smooth granite dome with distinct glacier-carved pinnacles rising from it.

According to popular folklore, the name "Kinabalu" originally came from "Cina Balu", which translates into "Chinese widow". Legend tells a story of a prince from China who ascended the mountain in search of a precious pearl. He then married a Kadazan (Sabah's largest ethnic group) woman but soon abandoned her and returned to China. His heartbroken wife wandered into the mountains to mourn and eventually turned into stone, becoming Mount Kinabalu. It's a sad story, but I felt it adds to the mysterious and elevated feeling you get from the mountain.

Mountain lovers definitely put Mount Kinabalu on their bucket list. But even people who aren't regular hikers like to give it a go, as it is considered one of the safest and most doable peaks in the world. The latter was the case for my friends. You see, when

I returned to university the following school year, invigorated by the climbing experience, I organised a climbing expedition for me and my friends. It actually started with a casual conversation that morphed into serious planning.

Organising was not so difficult since I knew the details from my previous trip. But I exercised extra effort to ensure the best experience possible for everyone. This is something I learnt from my parents and put it into practise. Having observed how well my parents look after visitors to our home, I followed what I saw them do. After we decided how many of us would be going, I rented a car and drove to the Kinabalu Park Headquarters over a weekend with two of my friends. They were joining the climb too. That very same day, we secured the climbing permits and sleeping places at Laban Rata, booked a van to transport us from our campus to the park, and booked a place to stay at the park the day before our climb. Having learnt from my previous experience, I convinced the group to spend an extra night at the park before the climb the next day as that would help us to start fresh. And although I found out after our trip, all the arrangements could have been done over the phone or by visiting the representative office at Kota Kinabalu, the additional trip to the Kinabalu Park Headquarters wasn't a waste, as at least I knew for sure, every important item was taken care of. My friends and I also had a good time exploring the park itself over that weekend trip. In life, additional efforts typically bring joy.

Due to my previous experience, it was an easier climb for me this second time. Before the trip, I took the time to reflect and honour my struggles during the first climb. I noticed what worked and what didn't. It was a powerful self-reflecting exercise. For example, I realised that my father and I had walked at a faster pace due to time limits, and we'd taken fewer but longer breaks. The second time, I reminded myself to use a different approach during the climb. I did the opposite. I moved at a slower but consistent pace. I also had quick water breaks more often. I didn't wait for my body to signal me to drink through thirst before reaching for my water bottle. The quick water breaks also helped me to get starting again more easily as my body had not cooled down that much. It's very much like a machine that needed to keep the momentum going. And, of course, I encouraged everyone in the group to do these same strategies.

Also, unlike what I'd done with my father, this time we ascended via the Mesilau Gate. It was a longer winding route up to arrive at the Laban Rata Resthouse, but because it was less steep than the path from the Timpohon Gate, it was easier. Of course, my friends, who were doing the hike for the first time, didn't know this, but I was aware of it.

Even with these changes to make it an easier and better trek, we had a different challenge this time. The weather was a bit wet. The on-and-off rain added challenges to the climb for the entire group. Some sections of the trail became slippery although I was grateful that everyone seems to be well-prepared with a pair of solid hiking shoes, including me. We all tried to make sure the important things like cameras, mobile phones, and our documents were well-protected from the rain.

Then I was wondering to myself, "If the rain continues, will we be able to proceed with summiting?" The rocky surface around the top, from what I remembered, would make the entire climb very challenging. Anyhow, there was no point thinking too much about this potential issue until the time came, I figured. The rain also lowered the temperature, and the fog became very dense, which impacted visibility in some sections. Nevertheless, it is always the rule that all climbers must hire a guide to walk in this park, and we had two, one guiding us at the front and another at the back. So we would be alright.

Even still, everyone was in high spirits. We took lots of photos (thank goodness we have photos this time!). We all made it to the Laban Rata Resthouse with plenty of time for exploration before dinner. How different the experience turned out than how it had played out for my father and me! I guess that's the wonder of an adventure.

Unfortunately, the next morning, one of my friends was not at her best. She decided not to continue to the summit. Most people would have pressed on, especially at this point where we'd come so far. But I actually admired my friend's courage for knowing herself and her needs, and raising a white flag. Her partner at the time decided to stay back with her as well. This all was decided in just a few minutes in the early morning before we left for the sunrise summit climb. The decision made by this couple touched me.

The rest of us pressed on, and we made it to the top. For me, reaching the peak this second time was a bit different. "Wow, I did it again! What's the next possibility for me?" I found myself wondering. Little did I know at that time, but later the universe would answer my question with a very big call.

I noticed that my greatest sense of achievement on this second climb of Mount Kinabalu wasn't because I made it to the top again. Instead, it came from organising and leading the "expedition". Fulfilling my role as leader was very satisfying.

Someone asked me, "Why did you climb it for a second time?" While many people might take it as something to tick off the bucket list after reaching the top and move on to look for the next item on the list, I looked at it differently. As human beings, we continue to look to challenge ourselves and take ourselves to the next level. But, it's not a competition with others. As I see it, it's more about bettering ourselves. I believe that's how we grow, and that's why I chose to climb it for the second time. The second time, I not only hiked it better, with more confidence, and practically zero worry about whether I could make it, I also did the organising to ensure my friends could experience the wonder and awe of the climb. In this way, it was a very different experience the second time. One in which I was able to better myself in a lot of different ways, mostly be putting in the effort to open the opportunity for dear friends.

Every time we move one step forward, we are one step closer to the level of excellence that we are aiming for. To give some perspective, I was in passive mode during the first climb. Dad initiated the climb and did all the organising, and I responded to it. It was a valuable experience even being passive. The second time, I switched to active mode. I initiated and organised the experience, not just for myself but for my friends too. I knew I would grow from it, and at the same time I also wanted to see how far I could take myself to help others extend themselves and experience the awe of a challenging and glorious experience.

Remember the question I asked myself while I was at the summit—"What's the next possibility for me?"—? A few years after my graduation from university, the universe presented me with an article about trekking in Nepal. Inspired by the article, I decided to add "trekking in Nepal" to my bucket list. While I didn't have any details on what this "trekking in Nepal" could mean, it gave me an overall direction to dream about—which, sometimes, is all you need!

2.
BLESSINGS THAT ARE HARDER TO SEE

*I will love the light for it shows me the way, yet I will
endure the darkness for it shows me the stars.*
—Og Mandino

I was born into a very good family that formed a solid foundation that shaped who I am today. I am always glad that I've never taken that for granted. Our family has long operated under a powerful principle, one that I still turn to: "Make a conscious decision to see the positivity from every event". I am always on the lookout for what I can learn. Every experience is a teacher, but I don't pretend all can be overcome easily, without any effort.

Cancer is a monstrous word. In the year 2000, my mother was diagnosed with cancer. She was 45. I was 16. At school, I was my usual self. I didn't want to talk about Mum's illness. While with the family, I asked myself not to add on any unnecessary burden by expressing my worries and sadness. It wasn't that I was super strong or that I knew how to handle the situation well by nature. I simply saw it as the best way that I could help my family. At a young age, I learnt that when something happens that I can't change, what I can do is choose my reaction. That's where my choice lies. And I can choose to react in a way that should help the situation.

If I told you that when my mother had cancer, that I wasn't scared, that it was easy to react in a way that helped the situation, or that it was not a struggle to "see the positive out of it", then I would be telling a big lie. But the positive did come … eventually. The thing I was able to ask myself to do was, no matter what, I'd be calm. I would do my best to keep a positive attitude.

At the same time, I acknowledged to myself that I had fear and I couldn't run away from it. The fear I had was around time—how much time did Mum have? Of course, I know that every one of us will come across the path of death at some point, and it's a matter of time. My grandmother passed away when I was 12. She was about 85. But my Mum's life timeline could be different. Much shorter. She was only 45 when she got cancer.

Mum was doing well with the treatments. Things seem to be heading in the direction that we were hoping for. Yet, deep down in my heart, I had a foreboding that Mum would soon cross death's path. And, she did. She died from cancer at the age of 50.

From 2000 to 2005, in those final five years we had with Mum, we cherished every moment we were together. Every family is unique and chooses to do things in its own style. For my family, there was always room for better. Sometimes, we still think about how it would be nice if Mum were still around to travel with Dad. It would be nice for my nieces and nephew to meet their grandmother. But we did what we could at the time. None of us is hung up on things that we did, or did not do, in the past and letting that impact our lives. We have good memories that are long-lasting. The important point I learnt from my mother's death to cancer at age 50, a point that I hope you take note of is—don't keep thinking that you still have a lot of time. When life takes a turn, you could lose your precious opportunity—the gift of being alive—forever.

When one of my sisters-in-law got killed in a car accident in the year 2012, our family was devastated. Again. Another untimely, tragic death. For a good couple of months, I was afraid to step into the shop where I'd received the call from my brother, asking me to go to the police station to find out if his wife was okay. At his request, I went to the nearest police station and provided as many details as I could. After the police officer made some calls, he turned to me to deliver the tragic news. My heart sank.

We actually experienced some blessings from that event, as the situation could have been worse. How? The greatest blessing is that my other brother and niece who were in the car accident as well—they both survived. My niece was found lying in a grassy area, away from the car, crying. We were told that most likely she survived because she wasn't trapped in the wreckage of the car. Other blessings too were the many people who helped along the way. The police officer who first arrived at the accident got in contact with a nurse who was passing by the scene. He coordinated that the nurse would bring my niece to the hospital. We also heard from the news that when car accidents happen, sometimes people pretend to help, but in reality they're looking to find out where the person involved in the accident lives, so they can rob their home because they know no-one will be there. None of that happened. Instead, all the valuables and important documents were handed back to us. We do not know all who were helping, but we are deeply grateful for their acts of kindness.

Although there were blessings, it still was an awful and sad tragedy. As I see it, even when trying to follow the family motto, "Make a conscious decision to see the positivity from every event", it does not mean I deny the facts. Rather, I find it most helpful when I take the courage to face the facts, even when they are incredibly sad and painful.

I was finally able to process the entire tragic event when I took the courage to step into the shop again, the shop where I received the call from my brother. I got along really well with my sister-in-law. It hurt when I realised that I would never be able to know her in a deeper, more personal way. She made a positive impact on me, and so did Mum.

These two terrible losses have helped me to cherish the time I have with my loved ones. They also act as constant reminders to me not to delay in making any form of contribution while I still have this life. This, to me, is very important.

So my wish for you is that you don't have to go through many painful experiences to realise how vulnerable and precious life is. I share this with the hope to guide you to start thinking about what is important in your life. And what is not. How you can make your life count. We are moving toward the same destination in terms of our present life, but who you are on the journey and how the journey and the ending will play out can be very different based on the many decisions we make during our lifetimes. Helen Keller said, "Life is either a daring adventure or nothing".

So, what stories are you going to tell the next generation? I will let you answer that for yourself and for the people you love.

3.

MORE THAN JUST SIGHT-SEEING

Travelling—it leaves you speechless, then turns you into a storyteller.
—Ibn Battuta

I am forever grateful for every decision, every event, and every person that crosses my path. Yes, that includes the not-so-good ones. Travel is actually the best reflection of that. When travelling, we are away from our comfort zone. No matter how much we plan, a less-than-ideal situation can still happen. For example, say, there's a workers' strike or a national holiday or a political demonstration, so all transportation is cancelled. Or no accommodations are available. You might get violently sick from food poisoning or a pickpocket might nab your wallet in a busy train station.

When something bad happens, I try to ask myself, "Is being angry going to help? If not, then how can I change my attitude to resolve or handle this situation? What can I learn in this situation?" I learnt to ask myself these questions the hard way.

Let's go back to my earlier story when I climbed Mount Kinabalu with my father. Recall that we arrived at the Laban Rata Resthouse late. We were hungry, tired, and all we wanted was to get some sleep. So we were in a "hurry mode" and had lost our focus about certain things. Dad ended up leaving my pouch in the dining area, of course, without realising it. What's so important about this pouch? It held important documents, like my national ID card. Dad had even offered to carry the pouch for me to keep it safe, so that I could concentrate on the climb and not worry about the possibility of losing it, yet he was the one to lose it!

We proceeded with the climb, woke early in the morning, climbed up to the summit, back down to the base, and all the way back to Kota Kinabalu. While we were unpacking, still feeling triumphant from completing the trek, I asked, "Pa, can I have my pouch back, please?"

Dad reached into his bag. When I saw him clearing everything out from it, my heartbeat raced. I shouted in my heart, "No, it can't be!"

He couldn't find it. He tried to recall where he could have left it. Then, he remembered. At the Laban Rata Resthouse, he'd been clearing things out of his vest to lighten the weight. He reckoned that's where he'd forgotten it.

"How am I going to get my pouch back? It's not like we can drive up. It took us more than seven hours to trek from the base, not including the driving distance from Kota Kinabalu to the base". Although I did not say any of this out loud, my expression said it all. Then the situation got worse when I finally said, "I shouldn't have given you the pouch".

Let's stop here and think through this. My father offered to take over my responsibility (my pouch). I accepted the offer. I was appreciative when he made the offer. Next, when a bad thing happened, I distorted the situation and acted like he'd "forced" me to give him the pouch. And to make things worse, I'd thought that gave me the right to blame him.

When we travel, we are in search of positive experiences. We want less or no negative experiences at all. But, this goes back to the fact that no matter how well we plan, things happen, and it is how we deal with it that shapes the experience.

In response to my accusation, Dad had every reason and the authority to be angry, but he chose not to be. Instead, he asked me, "San, is getting upset going to help with anything?"

His response took me by surprise. Yet, I was thinking in my heart, "Why am I expected to stay cool?"

Dad continued, "In life, you will encounter many similar situations to this one. Is that the attitude you will take when handling them?"

That got me thinking. When I was younger, most of the time I did not understand why my parents made me think so hard. I didn't understand why they didn't just come out and directly say whatever it was they wanted me to realise.

Later on, though, I realised that if they'd simply told me, most likely I would never have listened. When I come to a conclusion on my own, the effect roots in me more strongly, and I am open to change. And growth.

If you know me now, I hope the old-me, the one that got upset at my father over the pouch, does not scare you off. And yes, that was me. I'm still not perfect and will never be. But I will continue to acknowledge when I am wrong. I will continue to commit to taking actions to change. It's hard. It takes time. There is no easy or quick way (although some can be easier than others). But, if you are willing to put in the effort, you will be able to come out from a situation with a better version of yourself. That's what I have experienced.

By the way, in case you are curious to know what happened to my pouch: after I took in my father's wise questions and cooled myself down, my brain was able to work better. We went to the park reservation office in Kota Kinabalu to ask for their help. And guess what? They were just about to contact us too. Apparently the staff at the Laban Rata Resthouse had found the pouch and handed it over to one of the porters to bring down to the base in Kota Kinabalu. The people at the park reservation office managed to trace my contact details from the climber registration (they knew to look for me as my ID card was in the pouch).

An invaluable event. I was very grateful. It also proved one thing to me: when facing a challenge, try to stay calm. Next, think through the situation. Most of the time you will find a solution. There is no benefit at all to being grumpy or complaining. As not only does it not do any good, but also it drags you down into a deeper negative zone. Sure, there will be times when you give in to the grumpiness and negativity, but my aim is as often as possible to try to rise above and not give in to frustration. Again—as often as possible!

I am fortunate to have been born into a family that loves to travel. Growing up we had numerous family road trips. For instance during school holidays, we travelled to Dad's hometown, Kuala Dungun, to visit Grandma. Kuala Dungun used to be an iron mining town in the 1940s. The iron ore was mined in Bukit Besi, a small town located inland to the west, and Kuala Dungun, located on the coast, served as the port to transfer the ore. At that time, a railway line was available to connect the two towns. The railroad not only served the mining industry but also villagers who used it as public transportation. Unfortunately when the mines gradually closed down in the late 1970s and early 1980s after the iron was exhausted, the rail service stopped. Kuala Dungun then found its survival in fishing activities.

When we were kids, we visited Grandma in her wooden house in Kuala Dungun. It was connected to my uncle's house (Dad's younger brother). On some mornings, I would eagerly wait for the magic door (the door that connected the two houses) to open that indicated the start of the wonderful playtime with my cousins. Other times, we would be out visiting other relatives or visiting places where my father used to spend time during his childhood. Like the place where he caught crabs (not for eating though, as these were tiny crabs) and where he swam with his friends. Speaking about swimming, Grandma's house was within walking distance of the beach. There, on some late afternoons, we would spend quality time exploring the seawater, like my father had done when he was a kid. And I particularly enjoyed the moment when evening approached, for that was when, beyond the ocean, the whole horizon got covered in orange as the sun slowly retreated, with the fishing boats resting quietly in the water after a maybe fruitful day. This scene always gave me a sense of calm.

Grandma's wooden house has since been torn down, along with many others in the area. Some have been replaced by concrete houses. My uncle has also moved to a concrete house not far from where Grandma's house was. The houses may have gone, but the memories stay.

From our last visit, the few rows of old shop houses standing in the town centre were still there. Hopefully they can withstand time and not get replaced, as I felt they were the identity of the little town. Nowadays, Kuala Dungun is known as the gateway to reach the famous island called Tenggol Island, which attracts many divers and island lovers during the non-monsoon seasons. Tenggol is about one hour away by speedboat from Kuala Dungun's jetty. The yearly visit of the leatherback sea turtle has also contributed to the economy of Kuala Dungun.

In those days from my childhood, there were no expressways to get to Kuala Dungun. We would travel from town to town, city to city. Some we could bypass, some we couldn't. It could take us up to nine hours to travel the 400 kilometres from where we lived to Kuala Dungun. So, what did Mum and Dad do to make the long road trip special? We used those towns and cities as pit stops to rest. Taking meals at our favourite places. Among them that carved a deep memory for me was a roadside stall in Kuantan (a town in the Pahang state), which sold ABC ("air batu campur", which means "mixed ice"), a perfect dessert for hot weather. As Malaysia is located near the Equator, it is hot and humid throughout the year there. And the roadside stall was set up right under a big tree, which served as the perfect shelter. Unfortunately during our last trip, the big tree had been chopped down to give way to a wider road, and we couldn't find the stall anymore.

A Chinese restaurant called Tong Juan in Kemaman was another favourite stop for us. Their specialty was stuffed crabs. What I like the most were the fillings they used to stuff the crab shells, like crab meats and other vegetables, but no pork as I'm not a pork-lover. Sometimes, if we missed the timing and the stuffed crabs were sold out, I would shout in disappointment in my heart. Luckily they had other good dishes to fill my disappointment (just a little bit). Stuffed crabs were such a specialty.

In Kemaman, there was also a coffee shop called Kemaman Kopitiam where we would stop for a break. My parents would go for coffee, and we children would go for Milo. Since I've become an adult, I have ditched Milo and now go for a cup of ice coffee. Malay coffee is a bit different from Western coffee. The "kopi susu", or "milk coffee", that I like has condensed milk in it. And it is my favourite combination to couple it with butter-and-"kaya" (a type of jam) toast.

Sometimes we'd even stop for a "nasi lemak", a Malay fragrant rice dish cooked in coconut milk and pandan leaf, wrapped in the banana leaf in a triangle shape. I seemed to have a particular fondness for some other east coast foods like the puff. In the state of Johor where I was born, the puff is normally stuffed with potatoes or chicken, and the one I like, which is found in Kuala Dungun, is stuffed with fish. And the fish cracker made in Kuala Dungun has more fish than flour. Being close to the ocean, it makes sense that the foods from Kuala Dungun have this fish component that I love.

Other than food stops, having a bit of play at the beach or a swim was also part of the itinerary. Teluk Cempedak ("teluk" means "bay", and "cempedak" is the name of a fruit) and Rantau Abang ("rantau" means "region", and "abang" means "older brother") were among the two beaches that we visited often. My fondness of the ocean may have started from here. I cultivated a different swimming style because swimming in a pool and swimming in the ocean to me are quite different because of the different densities of the water. Swimming in a pool gives me a sense of security, and the ocean provides me a sense of adventure. From these childhood beach visits I was able to see the different types of seashells and tiny fish, even just in the shallows of the ocean water. It was always exciting.

Also during this time, Dad was driving his old Mazda. There was no built-in music player, so Mum packed up a portable radio, cassettes, and batteries so that we'd have music along the journey. American classics, like John Denver's "Take Me Home, Country Roads" and The Cascades' "Rhythm of the Rain", and Chinese classics, like Teresa Teng's "The Moon Represents My Heart", were among the songs we loved. My love of music grew on these road trips, and music made the travelling so pleasant.

Malaysia is not a big country, but I must admit that I have not been to every corner of my home country. We were regular road travellers along the east side of the West Peninsula because it was part of the journey to visit Grandma. From the south where we were located towards the north side, the cities that my family set foot in frequently were Penang and Melaka. In those times, there were no smartphones, so you relied a lot on road signs. In a more complicated travelling situation, a paper map might come into play.

But most of the time, Dad seemed to know the way. It was like he had a natural talent for remembering or figuring out directions, even if we did not visit a place often or even it was a new place that we were visiting. Like finding the way to Penang Hill that offered us fabulous panoramic views of Georgetown, the city centre of Penang, and Penang Bridge, which connects the island with the peninsular mainland. In Melaka, when we discovered Nyonya Makko, a restaurant that served delicious Nyonya food, we became loyal fans. Then closer to our home city, there is a fishing village called Kukup, known for its seafood restaurants built up on stilts over the water. I enjoyed very much traversing the boardwalks, for not only did they bring me closer to the water, but also I was able to observe more closely the many fish swimming freely below.

As I grew older, I started to understand that the road trips were more than just road trips. They taught me a lot of important life lessons. For instance, I learnt that there's an art to travelling. A big portion of that art rests on a lesson that I mentioned in a previous chapter: "When something not so great happens that you can't change, what you can do is choose your reaction". Of course, practising this lesson is more challenging than simply realising it. The practise is ongoing and applies to all areas of life.

By the way, I recall that my father had a lot of conversations with the locals on these road trips—when we stopped for petrol, when we had our meals at restaurants, when we bought fruits from roadside stalls, when we had our breaks at the coffee shop. Upon reflection, I believe these were more than casual conversations. Who else can provide better directions in navigating a town or city if not the locals? No wonder it seemed my father had an innate ability to locate places!

After I graduated from university and started my work life, I became the organiser of road trips with friends as my travel companions. I took my friends to the places where my parents had taken my brothers and me years earlier—out-of-the-way restaurants, unique and not-so-famous sites, and obscure villages and towns around West Malaysia. Revisiting these special places brought back sweet memories. "Wow, how do you know these places so well?" friends often asked me. I gave credit to my parents. They had the vision and understood what makes life special.

Our family's travelling was more than sightseeing. They were also informational expeditions. As an example, Dad would point out a landmark so that we could better remember the location of a restaurant. He would say, "One day, you may want to take your friends or your family here". How cool is that? Nowadays, of course, the internet has made the search for a place or a restaurant easier. But I will forever cherish those times.

4.

STEPPING UP TO THE NEW ENVIRONMENT

Life begins at the end of your comfort zone.
—Neale Donald Walsch

As noted in chapter one, I was still in secondary school when my parents moved to Sabah in East Malaysia for Dad's job. My brothers were already out of the family home, with my oldest brother working in Singapore and my other brother studying in Kuala Lumpur. I was 16 when my parents made the move, so I had two years of secondary school to complete, living on my own in Johor Bahru. I think this early start of independence helped me a lot down the road. For instance, most of my close friends were able to continue on into high school in the same school in Johor Bahru. My academic result wasn't good enough to continue in the same high school for the final two years, but I needed the final two years of high school in order to apply for a government university (which meant cheaper education fees than a private university). So I attended the only college which offered high school certification at that time and which accepted paid students. I moved to Kuala Lumpur to attend this college and get the high school certification. The early independence also gave me the experience of being responsible and the confidence in myself to go to university in East Malaysia where I ended up far from family and again on my own. It also set me up to be not just comfortable but eager to do solo travelling, even solo overseas travelling.

My first solo travel overseas was in the year 2011. I'd been thinking of joining an overseas volunteer trip. When I came across an organisation called Cross-Cultural Solutions (CCS), I signed up with one of their projects in Xi'an, China. By then, I was in my late-20s and had already been living away from home for a couple of years. I thought I was in a pretty good position to have support from my family to go ahead with the trip. To my surprise, my father did not accept my news of this service trip to China very well at the beginning.

The day I brought the news to Dad, he was picking me up from the bus terminal. I remember the excitement I felt when I was sharing my upcoming trip to Xi'an with him. I remember telling him I'd signed up with CCS and would be heading to China for a week to participate in a service program with a community in Xi'an. It would mean another level of volunteer experience, as CCS believed that through meaningful volunteer service, we could build relationships with local communities, which would then contribute to greater global awareness and appreciation of other communities and people. It would be a great birthday gift to myself for the year.

However, my father's equally excited and supportive attitude changed when he realised that I would be going by myself. "Why do you have to go by yourself? Can't you go with a friend or two? Have you done enough research on this CCS? How reputable are they?" Although I tried my best to answer his questions, my responses seemed to disturb him even more, so much so that he kept missing exits on the freeway home. That day, the less-than-30-minute drive home took us about two hours.

On one side was Dad with his serious concern about my safety in terms of going to China, a country that I had never been to before. On the other side, there I was, alone, confused, and upset that all the adventure, can-do, and embrace-the-challenge attitude and support he'd been giving me all my life seemed, in fact, very limited.

I should add that both my brothers supported me and didn't think there was a problem at all. In the end, their support influenced Dad to support me. But I had to agree to contact him every day to let him and my brothers know how I was doing. Now, you might be scratching your head and asking, "Why the worry?"

While I was growing up, I was somewhat exposed to the cultural differences between the East and the West. As an example, for us of Chinese descent (I'm a Chinese Malaysian), generally you don't leave home until you are married or if you are going to another city to study or work. It's a different situation for young people in Western cultures where it is common for young adults to leave their parents' home and live independently. And because of their independence, travelling, especially backpacking in a foreign country, is rather a common activity. But this is not standard in my culture. Once in a while, I did wonder if my spirit of adventure would give me enough courage to also try out backpacking in a foreign country by myself, especially when I saw young Westerners carrying backpacks and exploring lovely places in my home country. The thought quickly faded away because it's just not common within my culture.

As I shared previously as well, I grew up in a family that loves to travel. Notice though that we always travelled together as a family. I had the privilege to participate in a short-term student exchange program during my university studies. I visited Paris and London with my lecturers and other university mates. I've been to Stockholm with my father to visit my brother and his family who are living there. Notice, there was always someone else with me on these trips. Until I planned this service trip to Xi'an, I'd never been overseas by myself.

I always felt very blessed in my parents' approach to raising me. In fact, I think my father particularly cared that I would never underestimate my ability just because I'm a girl. He's always encouraging me that whatever my brothers do, I can do as well. Hence, I made an assumption that he would be supportive of my trip to China. After all, there would be someone from CCS meeting me when I arrived. However, being the youngest and the only daughter in the family, at that time, I did not take the time and effort to understand an important fact (which I understand now, again via the hard way): I will always be seen as the precious princess in my father's eyes, the one whom he will do his very best to protect. I would need to allow space and time for him to reach the point where he could have trust in me to do things like travel overseas by myself. Don't get me wrong, it was not that he didn't trust me, but it was about reaching that special point of knowing in his heart that I would choose to do the right thing, no matter what.

Also, it seemed my drastic approach of not having any discussions with him prior to my decision to travel to Xi'an added to the tension. After my mum passed away, for a good couple of years, I noticed there was typically a tension in conversations between me and my father. Later on, I reflected a lot and realised that Mum had always been the person whom I'd had the deeper conversations with. I didn't know what to do when Dad "suddenly" became that person. Our comfortable relationship of father and daughter was interrupted when I tried to talk to him on the deep level that I'd talked with Mum. Gradually, I chose to remain silent as much as I could because I disliked the tension that resulted when I tried to share more with my father.

I feel that our disagreement and his challenging me over my decision to go to Xi'an was a good thing. Through this disagreement, he and I came to have better and deeper conversations again. We were able to regain trust in one another through these conversations. Our relationship grew stronger and deeper.

While I'll share with you in some detail the fascinating volunteering aspect of this Xi'an trip in the next chapter, let me assure you that going to Xi'an was terrific. Even before going, I'd long been fascinated by China. As mentioned, I'm of Chinese descent. I love reading stories about the different dynasties in China. The starting point of that interest was actually relevant to my family's name, Song "宋" (in Mandarin), because the Song Dynasty was one of the dynasties in China's history. Our family name "Song" got translated to "Tang" in Malay due to the dialect that my grandfather was speaking and that the registration officer recorded in the official document. Coincidently, there was also the Tang "唐" Dynasty in Chinese history. There you go, that attracted my interest.

One more thing about Xi'an: it is the home to the Terracotta Army of Emperor Qin Shi Huang, who was the first Emperor of China (the Qin Dynasty). The Terracotta Army is a collection of terracotta sculptures representing the armies of Emperor Qin Shi Huang and is a form of funerary art that's buried with the emperor to protect him in his afterlife. What's even more fascinating is that the facial expression of each of the soldiers is different. How is that possible? According to the record, there are more than 8 thousand of them. Therefore, it was an eye-opening experience when I visited the museum myself. Though their colour may have faded, the part about the individual and unique expressions is true. Although the temperature of the museum was purposely kept at a lower level to protect the sculptures (there are also chariots with horses, cavalry horses, etc.), I was still able to feel the grandness of the atmosphere. It seemed to generate some form of warmth in me. It is said that the makers of the statues may have actually modelled the facial expressions from real people. That is unbelievable.

Xi'an, the city itself is rich in history, and that comes through significantly from some of the building structures that have been preserved. Imagine yourself sitting in a modern car on a modern road. You look out the window, and there it is, the Bell Tower of Xi'an, built in 1384. It doesn't even seem possible the two—the modern and ancient—could coexist.

A few years after this service trip to China, I applied and received an offer to work in Sydney, Australia. Dad's response: he was happy for me and proud of me too. He told me that when he heard the news, his spirits became so high that literally he began whistling as he walked. He noticed that I showed no hesitation in my decision to move to a new country that I'd never been to before. He actually agreed that my earlier decision to go to Xi'an helped me to make this bold move.

I moved to Sydney in October 2013. As I was on a four-year work visa, the time limit drove me to make serious efforts to explore Sydney and Australia itself as much as I could in the given window. On weekends, I asked myself to go out and explore one new place in Sydney neighbourhoods or even just around where I lived. I started off with an iconic landmark, like the Sydney Opera House, and shared that in a photo back home. Walking around the Royal Botanic Garden, which offers beautiful views of Sydney Harbour, gave me such a cosy feeling, taking in the breeze. A ferry ride to the Taronga Zoo and I met a real koala and kangaroo for the very first time (it was pretty exciting for me). I ended up visiting Cockatoo Island, which sits in the heart of Sydney Harbour. Formerly a convict penal establishment and reformatory school resided on the island. Next, the enjoyment of the ferry ride took me a bit farther, to Manly. Together with the bicycle that I rented at the time, I ended up at the North Head Artillery Lookout, and it was my very first time witnessing the exquisite high cliffs beside the ocean. These excursions opened up lots of possibilities for further exploration, followed by searches of where to go next, somewhere farther and yet close enough to make it a day trip.

Naturally, following the train lines was the best option for me. An approximately two-hour train ride to Katoomba took me to the Blue Mountains. My first time walking the Prince Henry Cliff Walk, accompanied by breathtaking valley views, drove me to go back again and again, taking on different walking routes, some into the heart of the valleys and the forest.

I also have a fondness of the ocean, so the Kiama Coastal Walk grabbed my attention. I did the north section, which I started from the Minnamurra Train Station and headed towards the Kiama Blowhole. It was my first experience to witness a blowhole. To me, it was like watching an orchestra playing by the ocean, and I was totally mesmerised by it. By the way, it is recorded that under certain sea conditions, the blowhole can spray 50 litres of water up to 25 metres in the air, quantities that can thoroughly drench any bystanders!

My explorations became bolder on long weekends. I would be more adventurous, heading farther away from Sydney. At the beginning, places along the train line were still pretty much my target. The very first place was Bathurst (approximately four hours by train from Sydney) where I spent my first Christmas in Australia. To be honest, I was a bit taken aback when I arrived in the town on Christmas Day. After I left the train station and walked towards the motel that I'd booked, following the Google map that I'd printed on paper (yep, you read it right. I wasn't using a smartphone at that time), literally there was no-one on the streets. It was like a dead city. Gulp. "Have I come to the wrong place?"

When I arrived at the motel, the owner was having Christmas lunch with her family and, at the same time, waiting for her only check-in guest of the day (me). I came to know later that most people were staying home celebrating Christmas with family and friends. Shops were closed, and I was the rare one who picked such a unique day to travel to this quiet town. The next day, I took a tour to some gold mines in Hill End. Again, I was the only one who'd booked, and John, the guide and tour operator, was kind enough to accept my booking. And because it was just me, instead of following the usual timing, John actually was happy to follow my pace. It was a pleasant Boxing Day although I did not find any gold.

The train line also took me to places like Dubbo, where I spent a night in the Dubbo Zoo itself. The most memorable moment was hearing the distant lion's roar in the middle of the night. I was glad I did not have a sleepless night though. Then to Coffs Harbour, where I visited the famous Big Banana Fun Park and toboggan for the very first time. It brought out the child in me. I also visited the Dorrigo Rainforest. I simply couldn't miss any opportunity that brought me closer to Mother Nature.

Gradually, the idea of renting a car and going on road trips was toying in my mind. I admit that I'm very glad that Australians drive on the same side of the road as Malaysian drivers. That makes the whole thing a lot easier.

Canberra became my first driving destination. After all, it is the capital city of Australia. I actually went farther on this drive, going to Thredbo where I got a little taste of walking one section of a trail that summits Mount Kosciuszko, the highest point in Australia. That extra adventure locked me down to return to complete the Kosciuszko Summit Walk. The rented car also took me to coastal towns like Forster and Port Macquarie via scenic routes. Driving itself brought me so much joy and reminded me that it is very much like life: we must enjoy the journey. It may take us time to reach our destination, so what we choose to do during the journey contributes to the reward awaiting us at the destination.

When you are new to a place, you can choose to act bolder as you are not limited by any precedent. You can be a bolder version of yourself. This is what I found for myself when I moved to Australia. For instance, I was told not to go bushwalk by myself for obvious safety reasons. Moreover, I was new in a foreign country. But it was such a huge temptation when I was at the Blue Mountains that very first time. I remember wondering, "How can I get on one of those tracks but not jeopardise my safety? I certainly don't want to play with luck here". Next, I saw a group of six people. They were in their bushwalking attire, and one seemed to be the leader, explaining something over a map. An idea came into my mind. "Maybe I can tag along with these people. Shall I ask? But I don't know them. Wouldn't they think I'm weird? Come on! So what if they think I'm weird? They don't know me anyway". So I took the courage to ask the leader where they were heading and if it was okay for me to tag along as I was by myself and very much want to explore the valley. After all, as it says in the Bible: "Ask, and it shall be given". And, by daring to ask, I got to join them and enjoy a bushwalk. The point is, if that day, I took the other version of myself to the Blue Mountains and was too shy to even ask, or too afraid of the answer no, I would have missed out on that bushwalk and likely many other opportunities as well. I probably would not be writing this book now for that matter.

On one occasion, I made a plan with a friend and her family to spend Christmas travelling Tasmania together. For those of you who don't know, Tasmania is a large, isolated island state off Australia's south coast. Tasmania is known for its areas of vast, rugged wilderness. It has wildlife, flora and fauna, that don't exist anywhere else in the world, like the Tasmanian devil. However, because someone got ill in my friend's family, they decided to cancel the trip. They invited me to spend Christmas with them at their home instead, but I figured that I would go ahead by myself to Tasmania. The car was already rented, and I only had to redo a few things on itinerary. I could even add in some hiking activities that we hadn't planned on doing because of my friend's children.

At the Launceston Airport when I first encountered the rental car, a Mitsubishi ASX, I found it was a bigger car than I normally would drive, and that caught me off guard a bit. But, of course, we'd needed a big car based on the number of people and the luggage from our original plan. I asked for a smaller car, also thinking maybe someone else could make better use of this big car, but it was the Christmas holidays, so all other cars were booked. I had two options: get over that barrier or cancel the rental.

So I went for it, saying, "Alright, Reddy (that's what I called the car), let's be nice to each other, shall we?" It wasn't as bad as I'd imagined initially. After a couple of good rounds of driving around the Launceston area, including visiting the Cataract Gorge Reserve, I was comfortable with the vehicle.

From Launceston I travelled to Bicheno, Wineglass Bay, Port Arthur, and Hobart, and I pocketed nearly a thousand kilometres in four days of driving. Reddy rested under some form of shade while

I met a Tasmanian Devil at the Bonorong Wildlife Sanctuary. I found the rare animal rather cute in its walking style.

What made the trip memorable for me was the drive up Mount Wellington in Hobart with Reddy. At certain sections, between us and the steep drop-off, there was only a single flimsy safety rope. Wow, it was precarious, but there was no way to turn around to drive down. At that point, I was so wishing again that Reddy was a smaller car. I had no choice but to keep going up, so I maintained my focus, directed the wheels carefully, and also watched out for oncoming traffic. There were cyclists too! I really took my hat off to them for cycling all the way up. I must say, as scary as it may seem now, it was worth putting out the courage to reach top and get to see the entirety of Hobart.

During the Tasmania trip, I was caught a number of times by unfamiliarity—with Reddy, with the winding roads, with the scary drive up to Mount Wellington. Several times I was out of my comfort zone. Reflecting on it now, I probably magnified things and got more concerned than I should have been. Perhaps it's easy for me to think this in retrospect since everything turned out well. And, getting out of our comfort zone is what grows us. It's among the gifts of travelling.

As I write this book, it is now my seventh year in this beautiful country of Australia. I continue pursuing the incredible travelling opportunities it offers. I continue to realise greater and greater personal goals and to challenge myself more and more to achieve those goals.

5.

THE ADVENTURE ATTITUDE

Life is a blank canvas, and you need to throw all the paint on it you can.
—Danny Kaye

The dictionary defines "adventure" as an "unusual and exciting or daring experience". Some people interpret adventure as engaging in risky activities, but I don't think that's necessarily true. There is no right or wrong answer. It all depends on the person and the type of stories they like to create and share with others. The more I taste the excitement of adventure, the more I want myself to be adventurous.

My first big adventure was at 6 years old when I went to Bangkok with Mum and Dad. We were with a tour group. The big adventure part of that trip was when I tried parasailing, the first time and only time so far that I've done it! People say that kids are fearless, I agree. And I'd like to add that kids are fearless because they don't have the prior experience to bind them. Also, they are at the stage of lots of learning and exploring. So for children, to make mistakes, fail, try again, and gain confidence and success is all part of the process. Therefore, it is also my wish if you have kids, that you encourage them, from a young age, to keep up their natural spirits and never get stuck in fear as happens to a lot of us adults.

When I was 6, I had the privilege to be one of the fearless kids. Of course, my parents played a critical role in helping me to taste the sweetness of adventure in smart ways, and I'm forever grateful to them for that.

About the parasailing: I can still see in my mind's eye the speed boat soaring along the ocean below us with "us" being me and the instructor, who was strapped in behind me, with the two of us up in the air held aloft by the parasail. "I believe I can fly. I believe I can touch the sky". Those are the lyrics from the song, "I Believe I Can Fly" by R. Kelly. At the age of 6, I did not know that song, but those were my feelings. When the wind brushed across my face while I was up in the sky, I first tasted the feeling of limitlessness and that would have a lasting effect on me.

While I was too young to observe it, I realise now there was a lot of trust going on in the parasailing experience. My parents entrusted me to the instructor whom they only spoke with briefly, but he must have given them the necessary trust and comfort. My instructor took the 6-year-old me up to the sky with him, and who knows how I would be reacting or whether I'd understand any of his instructions? As for me, trusting my parents, who would not take any chance to risk my safety, at the same time gave me an opportunity to have a little taste—oh no, I say, a big taste—of being bold. When we work together, it creates a wonderful experience for everyone. Too often as we go through adult life, we want to do things on our own and forget that a team can take us further.

There is no age limit in getting into an adventure either, which is another beauty of adventures. No matter your age, you can find the right adventure for yourself and go at your own pace. After all, it's not a competition. Take it as a challenge to yourself. In each challenge or adventure that you take on, just trying it means you've "won", so to speak. It is because you grow from the journey itself, which is priceless.

In 2016, Dad and I visited my oldest brother in Sweden where we went on a two-week road trip from Sweden to Norway. While we were in Norway, my brother, Dad, and I hiked the famous Pulpit Rock, also known as Preikestolen. With an elevation of 604 metres, it has an impressive view looking out over the Lysefjord. Lysefjord is the southernmost of the biggest fjords in Norway. The 40-kilometre-long fjord is flanked by steep mountains, some more than a thousand metres tall. The fjord is not only long and narrow, it is also, in places, as deep as the mountains are high. Only 13 metres deep where it meets the sea near Stavanger, the Lysefjord then drops to a depth of over 400 metres below Pulpit Rock. The fjords were formed by giant glacier tongues that shaped the landscape through several ice ages. It's like a U-shaped undersea valley and some of it is surrounded by dramatic mountain scenery.

My sister-in-law stayed back with my niece and nephew because the hike up Pulpit Rock would be a bit too challenging for the children. It is my wish that one day, they will get to witness the majestic views from the top with their own eyes.

Compared to our adventure climbing Mount Kinabalu, whose elevation and level of difficulty are much greater, the Pulpit Rock climb might seem like a walk in the woods. But my father was 69 when doing the Pulpit Rock climb. Dad walked at his own pace, honouring his body's particular walking rhythm, and reached the top and did the same on the descent. My brother and I decided to honour Dad by naming him the oldest person to summit Pulpit Rock. The oldest person, that is, from Kuala Dungun, Malaysia, the fishing town where Dad grew up, to summit Pulpit Rock! Yeah, go Dad!

Another source of adventure and magic for me that can also be high risk is scuba diving. When I graduated from university in Sabah, as a kind of congratulatory gift to mark the achievement, I wanted to go scuba diving. Of course, I'd need to get certified. As a new graduate from university who was just starting out in the working world, the cost to get certified would be a stretch for me financially. To make it a little bit more challenging, I also had the mentality (ego, if you will) that I should not be asking money from my father anymore. Because of this, it took a little bit of an inner struggle before I had the courage to ask him if I could borrow the money. As I already explained, Dad grew up in a fishing town, so he's no stranger to water activities. The ocean has a special place in his heart and mine too. As an appreciator of water activities and the ocean, my father already had his scuba certification (which I did not even know about it until that day), and he readily agreed and supported me in getting mine.

I find it almost ironic that while I'd just graduated from university, I almost failed the theory part of the SCUBA examination. I had to retake it before I could go on to take the practical part of the examination. Thank goodness I passed. Otherwise, I would have missed out on another great adventure—experiencing the underwater world of the ocean.

In my first dive into the ocean, it took some effort for me to stay just above the sea bed. I kept floating up and down, trying to control my buoyancy. Once I was able to stabilise myself a bit, that's when the magical moment happened. The quietness crept in. All I could hear was the sound of my own breathing through the regulator. Next, a school of fish swam in front of me and the instructor. This was the first time I saw fish in the water and was with them. Wow! After that, I spotted a clownfish while I was admiring the corals. Remember Nemo from the movie *Finding Nemo*? That's a clownfish! How great that first experience was.

As every adventure comes with a certain level of risk, I firmly believe that it is up to us, the adventurer, to manage the risk. So even after getting my SCUBA license, I make a point to take the refresher dive during my yearly diving trips. That is, to refresh my skills and remember the protocols before I go into deeper water. I choose to do this so that I can complete my dive safely. In turn, I will be able to better enjoy every magical moment while I'm in the deep blue ocean.

Dad always says, "Do your homework first, so that you are preparing for the good and also for the bad". I recall these words whenever I take on any adventure in my life.

6.

LET'S TALK: SAFE SELF, ADVENTURE SELF

Courage is not the absence of fear, but rather the assessment that something else is more important than fear.
—Franklin D. Roosevelt

It was a Thursday, 2 November, 2017. I was at home after a long day at work. After my shower, I sat down in front of my laptop to read through my emails. Another normal Thursday night. But, then, an email caught my attention. The subject read, "We're Climbing Mt. Everest and you are invited, Wei San". Tired, but driven by curiosity, I opened it and started reading through it. This was a two-part opportunity and challenge sponsored by UNICEF Australia: (1) trekking to Everest Base Camp and (2) fundraising AUD $4 thousand for UNICEF. Something magical happened—word by word, the message seemed to explode in my brain. As I processed the words, one of my dreams awoke inside me. Years earlier I'd had the general bucket list dream of hiking in Nepal, so this certainly fit the bill. I clicked at the link that said, "Download your information pack today". That was the life-transforming email and the beginning of an extraordinary journey.

"Hang on, you make it sound so easy", you might be thinking.

No, it wasn't so easy. Not at all. When I considered how much I wanted to do it, how excited and invigorated I felt about the possibility of it, I noticed someone creep into my mind. It was the other-me, the "safe me". Within a few seconds of the excitement, the "safe-me" started questioning my enthusiasm about pursuing this adventure.

Safe Me: Hmm, San, you sure about this?

Adventure Me: It sounds so exciting!

Safe Me: Yeah, yeah. Agreed. Sounds very exciting, but—you think we can do it?

Adventure Me: What do you mean? Yeah, I do.

Safe Me: Well, it's Everest Base Camp we're talking about here. Sure, many people have done it, but do you think *we* can handle it?

Adventure Me: [*Silent*]

Safe Me: It requires a lot of stamina—you do know that, right?

Adventure Me: I'm exercising. And I've hiked before. I've trekked Mount Kinabalu with an elevation of 4,095 metres, the highest peak in Malaysia—two times! Pulpit Rock, Norway. Mount Kosciuszko here in Australia. I'm no amateur.

Safe Me: Yes, but I don't think it's that type of trekking. And, when we are really honest—we aren't very consistent in our exercise schedule nowadays. I don't mean to be a downer, I just want to help you be realistic.

Adventure Me: Oh. [*Pensive*]

Safe Me: Okay, there's something else we have to discuss too. Fundraising. As I recall, fundraising has never been one of our strengths. We are more of a stay-behind-the-scenes type. We are very good at the supporting role. Fundraising needs us to be at the front. Soliciting! Persuading, sharing the cause. Opposite of what we're comfortable with.

Adventure Me: [*Downcast*]

Safe Me: Why put ourselves under unnecessary pressure? [*Takes a pause here.*] There's more—that important project at work next year, remember? Are we able to be away from work for a whole month? Why don't we wait a bit, until the timing is right?

Adventure Me: Stop!

Safe Me: [*Silent and shocked*]

Adventure Me: First of all, don't you realise that the "right" timing will never come? Look back. Do you remember the times when the "right" time arrived for us?

Safe Me: [*Stares down. Silent*]

Adventure Me: You don't. You know why? If we observe when the "right" time comes, it's only when we create that "right" time. We've never waited for it. Remember the day we took the courage to ask about transferring to work in Sydney and how that led to our application to fill a vacancy in Sydney? We did not wait for someone to make the offer. We took the steps by first expressing our interest. Then we got through the process. Imagine if we took the approach of waiting. Not only would people not know what we wanted, but we also wouldn't have given ourselves a chance to even try.

Safe Me: [*Still silent, but obviously listening*]

Adventure Me: Now, I know, the first step is always scary. But what's worse—to try and maybe not succeed, or, later in life, to regret not trying? [*A pause*] How do you eat an elephant?

Safe Me: What?

Adventure Me: I know, we don't eat an elephant. It's a metaphor. Now, before we can find the steps to eat an elephant, we first need to decide if we want to eat an elephant, right? Otherwise, why bother? Have you noticed, we work well when there is a goal to aim for. It's a pull factor. Look back again. Inspired by our oldest brother's move to Sweden, we said we wanted to go overseas to broaden our life experience too. That's the goal that led us to take action. We said years ago after we summited Mount Kinabalu that we wanted to go trekking in Nepal. Here comes an opportunity. Is there a strong reason for us to let go of this opportunity?

Safe Me: [*No response. But nodding head in overall agreement*]

Adventure Me: Look, this opportunity is waiting for us to grab it. Yes, there's a lot of effort that'll have to go into this. But think of all the positives. I can imagine that we'll have to learn to be patient, for training and fundraising take time. And guess what? We have the time—it's a year away! We'll learn to see the good, even in the uncomfortable moments. We'll push ourselves out of our comfort zone by doing new activities. And that's okay. That's great because the potential growth will be enormous.

Safe Me: [*Looks at the other with warm eyes and a cautious but apparent smile*]

Adventure Me: I need both of us to be on the same side to make this work. [*Pause*] What do you say?

Safe Me: [*Gives a small but decisive nod to mean yes*]

There is something to be afraid of everywhere around us. Some fears are created by circumstances, and some are created by us. The bad news—there is no magic spell to turn our world into one free of fear. Where there's nothing to be afraid of. When you think about it, a world like that is probably not as great as you'd think. The good news—every day, many, many people are doing brave acts, both large and small. They are demonstrating bravery that is inspiring and motivating to the rest of us. What then makes some people act anyway, even if they are afraid, while others get knocked down by even a small fear?

In my personal experience, when I am courageous, I carry on even in the face of fear. It's not like courage means no fear. That's not it at all. I've come to expect that when I enter the world of uncertainty—where real adventure often lies—the feeling of fear creeps in too. Fear actually comes knocking on the door first before the other feelings—exhilaration, wonder, awe, gratitude. When I am courageous, I recognise my fear. Then how I choose to act anyway becomes the key.

Courageous people understand that being brave is not equal to having no fear. They choose to move forward and overcome that fear in pursuit of a bigger and greater purpose. Something so big that they are willing to face that fear monster and have a fight with it. After all, there is no fear to overcome if there is none in the very first place, which means no adventure and staying in their comfort zone.

Now, how to do that? I am a firm believer that action is the best antidote. The more we do, the more we know. The more we know, the more we have the power to talk ourselves up and through the fear. To act anyway. When we act anyway, it becomes less scary than we thought. Then after a few more tries, it gets smoother. By that time, we leave the fear behind. I actually argue that because the feeling of fear is universal and necessarily something every single person must contend with, fear is a kind of gift that allows us to develop ourselves.

To start an adventure journey, the first major fear hurdle to jump is simply determining our destination. Otherwise, we remain idle in our comfort zone, just dreaming, and the aimless dreaming of the so-called future adventure is the end in itself. We are not challenged. Nothing happens. So, the first dose of courage is the courage to make a decision to engage an adventure.

When I was less courageous and let fear keep me in place, a common excuse I'd use with myself was—"I will do it when the time is right". As all of us know already, the "right" time never comes. No matter who we are, a billionaire or not, we all only have 24 hours a day, 365 days a year. How we use that time is what varies, and that is the decision we can make.

I came to realise that I have the "ability" to make the timing right. And the first step that brought me there was actually allowing myself to follow my heart's calling and taking the courage to make the decision—to commit to the UNICEF Australia challenge. So, even though I did not sign up for the challenge that very night, I laid out a very strong foundation for myself for all the reasons that it would be a difficult but also a fabulous adventure for me. I remember going to sleep with a big smile on my face. Wild dreams entered my sleep. Heaps of imagining where this adventure would take me!

In case you have the question, "How do I make things happen, especially something that's big or looks scary? Should I tell people around me about my goal?"

My standard approach has been the opposite—when I have a big goal, I don't talk about it with others. At least not until I've made some progress. But I realise that I tend to keep quiet out of fear—fear of failing people who care about me if I don't end up doing it. I am also afraid of failing myself. I have been very cautious in many areas of my life. While sometimes this kind of caution and quiet pursuit of my goals has helped me achieve great things, I realise that it also has a downside. I'd even say it's prevented me from trying new things. When that happens—when my "safe self" tries to stifle my "adventure self" so that keeping things to myself does not work, that's when I've learnt to give an extra push to strengthen my will and the adventurous side of myself.

In the case of this Everest Base Camp trek, I knew I needed more resolve, so the day after I got the email, I shared my intention of signing up for the challenge with a colleague when I was at work. The weekend at marching band rehearsal—yes, I'm a piccolo player in a marching band—I shared my goal with my band manager. Over the same weekend, I even talked to my family about the goal.

And how did all these others respond to me? Support. Everyone gave me warm, enthusiastic support. So, I jumped the fence!

And once I made the decision, everything else seemed to be easier. Manageable even.

7.

A HEART OF GIVING

It's not how much we give, but how much love we put into giving.
—Mother Teresa

As mentioned, it was UNICEF Australia that we were fundraising for by trekking to Everest Base Camp. A little background on the organisation: it has programs that help vulnerable children. It's their aim to protect and improve the lives of children. As it says on the website, "UNICEF is the world's leading organisation working to protect and improve the lives of every child in over 190 countries" and "We protect and advocate for the rights of every child in Australia and overseas. We provide life-saving support and protection for children during emergencies and crises. We deliver long-term international development programs, including education, nutrition, and health care".

Personally, I'm a huge education advocate. To me, it's very important for every child to receive a good education to reach their full potential. It's the good education I received that allowed me the many opportunities I've had. Thus, I became a UNICEF Australia supporter.

Supporting a charitable organisation like UNICEF Australia is something I've been wanting to do since I was a child. Really, it was my parents who led me and my brothers by example, showing us the importance of helping others. They even encouraged me to get involved as a volunteer from a very young age.

There was a period of time when I was in primary school that Dad limited the amount of time I could watch television. It was an hour a day, so I had to choose carefully the program that I would watch. One of my favourites was a Hong Kong drama series. It told the story of two doctors. One of them worked in a well-known private hospital and the other in a government hospital in Hong Kong. An assignment with Médecins Sans Frontières (MSF) brought them together in Kenya. Some episodes of the show were pure entertainment, but the one where they met in Kenya through MSF was not one of those. In case you don't know, MSF is a real organisation, not just one on a TV show. It is an independent medical humanitarian organisation that provides emergency medical aid to those affected by armed conflict, epidemics, healthcare exclusion, and natural or man-made disasters. What I saw the doctors on the TV show do via MSF made such a huge influence on me that I hoped to join MSF in the future. At that time, I thought becoming a doctor was the only way.

So, I joined the Red Cross while I was in primary school as part of my extracurricular activities. At that young age, I wasn't learning so much about how to provide first aid during emergencies, but it was more towards the soft skills side of things. During an emergency, what do you do? Remain calm, do not panic, and get help—that type of knowledge. The other aspect was around discipline. When you are in the uniform, you represent the organisation behind the uniform. I learned to take my uniform seriously and that led me to take my behaviour seriously. It started while I was in uniform, and that influenced me even when I wasn't in uniform.

As an example, coupled with the upbringing from my parents, I learned to respect time a great deal, my time and other people's time. Punctuality is embedded in me.

In high school, I chose to join the St. John Ambulance. Through this organisation, I got myself into a more serious mode of learning first aid knowledge. We got to apply what we learnt through simulation competitions, within our school or between schools. Through events in our own school or inter-schools, like Sport Day, Open Day, etc., I got to join others to be of service and on standby in case of emergency. Although I never had any experience with major injuries during my time of service, it was still valuable because the seniors showed us many tips on what to look out for. For example, a marching parade was part of most of the events, and as the marchers stood under the sun, waiting for the parade to begin, we learnt to keep our eyes open for those who might be showing signs of fainting due to dehydration. We wanted to reach them before it actually happened.

As far as studying medicine went, because I wasn't doing that well in my high school classes, I had to drop the subjects that are mandatory for those who hope to study medicine at university. In that way, I gave up my ambition of becoming a doctor. What's great for me is how it led me to discover other paths for helping others.

After Mum passed away with cancer, I was determined to help others battling cancer. The day I walked into Cancerlink Foundation's office while I was still in Malaysia, I wasn't sure what or how I could contribute. The founder of the organisation was at the office that day. As we chatted, I learnt that she founded the organisation after her husband passed away from cancer. She wanted to help anyone who crossed paths with cancer, whether they themselves had it or someone close to them. She believed that relieving any pressure from those affected could help them to focus on the treatment itself. When I left the office that day, I became one of their newsletter translators, something I volunteered to do for several years.

While I was with Cancerlink Foundation, I also had the opportunity to help out in one of their weekend camps for children. The camp was for children ages 7 to 15 who had cancer. During the camp, I was one of the team leaders. We had so much fun doing all kinds of activities with the children. We led the children on a 20-minute walking trail into the forest. It was short but ideal for them, allowing them to be with Mother Nature. We played team-building games like traffic jam and human knot. We had a performance night, which allowed the children, including the team leaders, to perform something together as a team. That night, new or almost forgotten dreams and boldness became realised through songs, storytelling, acting … It was so inspiring to see the children immersed in the moment as if cancer had never come into their lives at all.

At the end of the camp, the team leaders gathered in a circle at the centre of the hall. We all had our eyes closed. I was a bit nervous as we were not told about this activity. Next, someone came close to me and whispered words into my ears. Another person came and whispered. And another. The words were short and sweet messages from the children on my team. As their thank-you messages travelled into my ears, my heart melted. I had tears rolling from my eyes. I thought I'd been giving something to the children and not asking for anything in return. And yet, how much the children had taught me in return with their marvellous fighting spirits. That weekend made me realise, even more, how blessed I was. And am.

From that weekend camp, I first had the idea of doing an overseas volunteer trip. I liked the idea of "travelling with a purpose". To me, it meant a fuller experience of the people and places visited, forging stronger connections with locals. Be it going to places where the locals go or involving myself in local community activities or projects. While searching for suitable volunteer-type travel opportunities, Cross-Cultural Solutions (CCS) crossed my path. They work to address critical global issues. As their website states: "CCS believes that through meaningful volunteer service we can build relationships with communities that are essential components to increased tolerance and global awareness". At the same time that CCS volunteers provide services to communities, the volunteers also contribute to the local economies. After more detailed research, I decided to sign up with one of their programs in Xi'an, China, as already mentioned in the book.

During my one week in Xi'an, a group of corporate people from the United States were doing the same CCS mission with me. Our group was further divided into smaller groups, and I joined the group and went to a primary school that provided education to children with special needs. Despite the reading material provided before my arrival and the briefing session given by the program manager, I was a bit nervous. Before the start of the first day, I reminded myself to have an open heart and an open mind. And the warm welcome and support provided by the school staff relieved my worry. They were very friendly. I also felt they wanted to help volunteers like us to settle in. Moreover, it's the universal law—an open heart invites open hearts.

It was a valuable week. It helped me to reflect on many areas of my life. The group of children I worked with deserved a good education, as much, perhaps even more so, than their peers who did not have special needs. True enough, these children needed to go the extra mile and also needed extra support, but that was okay. I was very impressed with the school staff, the local community, and organisations like CCS that provided the extra support, patience, and care for the youngsters.

I met one young teacher whose passion was very inspiring to me. Also her determination in choosing her career, especially at her young age, impressed me. She wasn't doing her work just to make a living. Helping her students with special needs was her calling. Ralph Waldo Emerson said, "Every man I meet is my superior in some way. In that, I learn of him", which I more than agree with. The wonderful young teacher with her great spirit, as well as many others, showed me that "the secret to living is giving", like what Tony Robbins said.

When I arrived to live and work in Sydney, as a newcomer in a new country, I figured that doing some volunteering would help me to settle into the new environment. Also, it would provide me with the opportunity to engage with local communities. One particular day, I was heading towards Coles, a supermarket, when I noticed a booth in the foyer for Starlight Children's Foundation. What caught my attention? A child with a big, wide smile. A lady in a starship captain costume. A statement that read, "Brightening the Lives of Sick Kids", the mission statement of Starlight Children's Foundation. It brought back memories of my trip to Xi'an and the children at the weekend camp with Cancerlink Foundation. I ended up joining the Starlight Express Room (SER) program as a volunteer.

The SER program runs in hospitals. It aims to take away any fear sick kids have towards hospitals. The lesser the correlation between the hospital and a scary place, the better it is for the children. Also, while a sick child is getting their parents' full attention, their healthy sibling(s) may not be. It's not the intention of any parents; it's just because the illness is too much to handle. So, SER also aims to be a fun place for siblings and friends. And even a place for the parents to relax a bit. Every day, "captains" travel from the "Starlight Planet" to bring fun. It's all about having fun in a safe environment.

As volunteers, we help captains run the room. The focus is on the children. Be it helping the children by doing crafts, playing video games, watching movies, playing board games—the children make the call. I played Mario Kart for the first time during my first shift in the SER. I didn't even know how to operate the player, but it didn't matter to the children I was playing with.

While I was a bit involved with volunteer organisations growing up—the Red Cross and St. John Ambulance—I'd say my volunteering journey had its most profound start with Cancerlink Foundation. It showed me the positive energy that volunteering can generate. The trip to Xi'an with Cross-Cultural Solutions brought it to another level. Starlight Children's Foundation enhanced the experience. I became more confident, more ambitious, and more eager to play a bigger role and do more to give back to society with each new experience. These experiences set the stage for me to be open to UNICEF Australia's double opportunity and double challenge: trekking from Lukla to Everest Base Camp and fundraising. Of course, I'd heard inspiring stories about others who aimed to do a big challenge and raise funds for a good cause at the same time. But, to be honest with you, dear reader, what most scared me wasn't the 13-day trek ascending ~2,500 metres (and then descending it too!), all the while at an altitude where the oxygen levels would be drastically lower than humans are accustomed. Nope. It was the other aspect of the challenge that put fear in my heart: fundraising AUD $4 thousand. By the way, this excludes other aspects of the expenses like travel costs, equipment costs, participation fees.

Be it a success or a failure, I knew that I was going to give it a go. No regrets!

8.

JUMPING OVER THE FENCE OF FUNDRAISING

Change your thoughts and you can change your world.
—Norman Vincent Peale

I decided to look straight into the eyes of one of my fears and not run away. The fear—fundraising. Before I tell you more about this fear and how I tackled it, let me give you some background about me at this time in my life.

By this time, I'd been living and working in Sydney going on four years, and frankly, I'd allowed myself to get too comfortable. I stopped learning or pursuing new experiences and big, new adventures. I allowed the routine to overrun me. Initially, it started because I wanted a break from the constant challenging, learning, and growing. And that's legit. We're allowed to take rest breaks.

But I ended up extending and extending again that rest break, so it became a long one. And I ended up losing my spark. Losing that feeling of magic and mystery and awe and appreciation I usually felt in regard to life. I got complacent. It happened without me even realising it, and it's a pretty terrible feeling.

When we choose to do the easy things, life actually gets harder. Don't believe me? Take a moment to answer this question: do you feel more excited, more positive, and more energetic when your life is in the static mode or the opposite mode? For me, it's the latter. My decision to engage the Everest Base Camp challenge added spark to my life again. It was a year away, and there was so much I had to do. Including, looking straight into the eyes of the monster awaiting me.

Fundraising was that monster. It was my biggest deterrent regarding the challenge, but I just couldn't allow myself to give in or give up.

Some people love fundraising. Some people don't mind it, and they'll do it. Other people avoid it. I'm that type—I avoid fundraising. Before this challenge, the time fundraising came up in my life was when I was in high school volunteering for St. John Ambulance. St. John's operations and activities depended solely on the generosity of the public, government grants, and corporate sponsorship. Flag Days (which normally last for a month) are among the fundraising events where members and officers are mobilised into groups, wearing uniforms and St. John t-shirts, to appeal for donations. We'd go from house to house, at shopping complexes, and other public places requesting donations. We were entrusted with donation tins, and those who donated got a small flag or sticker. Other than that fundraising, I did my best to avoid any other fundraising.

I was a great support crew person, but it had to be behind the scenes. Staying behind the scene was my sweet spot. Was I too shy to ask for a donation? No, I did not think so. Then, what was my problem with fundraising?

It had something to do with protecting trust. The trust that I'd built among my circle of people—family, friends, colleagues, and such—over the years. Oftentimes people choose to do something—like donate money to someone else's cause—simply because they trust the person asking for the donation. I was always cautious when it came to the subject of money. I would not want to lead my circle of trusted people into any unpleasant experience with their money. Perhaps, I was too cautious, but I believed my concern was valid.

A well-functioning not-for-profit organisation *likely* manages its donation well. It is likely conscientious and transparent with a high percentage of every dollar going to the programs and people in need, and not to administrative matters. But, there are many examples of irresponsible people, in the name of charity, who have misused donations. Donations collected from kind-hearted people for people in need. There are many examples where organisations have poorly managed their donations, whether it be because they were sloppy and disorganised or due to greed. I call them the rotten apples. Most of the time, the rotten apples are the ones that get the public's attention, which makes it harder for those who are doing the right things, who are legit and truly helping people in need.

So, what got me to jump over the fence and face my fear of fundraising? A bigger purpose. I shifted the focus away from me, i.e., *I'm not good at fundraising*, to the greater purpose, i.e., *this is an opportunity for contributing to improving the lives of vulnerable children*. In doing so, I became more courageous and more willing to at least give it a try. I should add that it helped too that the greater purpose was associated with a well-known, well-respected international organisation. I believed that people would be receptive and generous to my campaign because they'd recognise the good reputation and work of UNICEF.

The particular area of UNICEF that these funds would go to was UNICEF's early childhood development program. Here's some background on it: from conception to the start of school is a critical period for a child. The program offers interventions that combine nutrition, protection, and stimulation for children. Those are the important ingredients of healthy early childhood development. As far as nutrition goes, the program delivers the proteins, fats, vitamins, and minerals that expectant mothers, newborns, and infants need. It delivers ongoing nutritional training and healthcare to parents and communities to ensure children thrive into adulthood. It works to ensure that all parents, caregivers, and communities understand the importance of stimulation for children. How are they promoting that? Through a range of activities, including the use of play, reading, and singing. They also work to provide quality early learning opportunities for all children. Because I could understand the significant benefits this program was offering and I believed in the power of the work that UNICEF did, I figured that others would too, which would make my fundraising efforts manageable, at the least, and fruitful and fun, at the most. At least, that's what I hoped!

And, time was on my side too. I had the time to plan and execute the plan to meet my fundraising target of AUD $4 thousand. Yes, it was a large amount to commit to raising. That's another reason why the fundraising aspect brought me such anxiety from the very beginning. But guess what? On my fundraising webpage, I set the target to AUD $5 thousand. "What? Are you out of your mind?" you're asking. Nope! In fact, having a higher, bolder goal turned out to be an even stronger motivation for me, because, as Les Brown said, "If you shoot for the stars, you're at least going to hit the moon". So, instead of saying, "I can't do it", I asked myself, "How can I do it?" When you change your words, it changes how your brain thinks. It flips your mind from a close state to an open state, and that opens up more possibilities.

Okay, time to admit a little secret here. I updated my fundraising target on my webpage a couple of times. I started with AUD $4 thousand, then moved it to AUD $5 thousand. Later, I moved it back to AUD $4 thousand because I was doubting myself. Then, after that, I moved it back up to AUD $5 thousand and asked (begged) myself not to change it again.

That was when I realised I needed to ask for help.

Most of the time, I ask myself to be independent. To try not to bother others. To resolve any situation on my own first. Generally, doing things in this way reinforces itself so that I become more capable and more independent each time I succeed. Yet, at the same time, it also results in me avoiding things that I'm not good at because I'm too shy to ask for help. I'd say that I've missed out on things in life, including exciting things, because of my reluctance to ask for help. This is another reason why fundraising was scary to me—the only way to fundraise necessarily entails asking others for something—but it also presented an obvious method for growth.

Having to fundraise actually surprised me in that it cleared a lot of my misunderstanding about asking for help. The experience was actually pleasant. The amount of support I received, during my fundraising, from others was enormous. Having said that, I did receive rejections. I was afraid of rejection when I first started, but when it happened, I was actually okay with it. The rejections usually were accompanied by words of affirmation and encouragement. It was another form of support.

If you wonder what I asked myself to do to move forward with the fundraising piece, here are some stories. The very first step was following the instructions in the registration packet and setting up my fundraising page on a website called "Everyday Hero". There I outlined my fundraising goal and my story of why I was doing this particular fundraising challenge. This was really the easiest part. Next was how to let people know. I was never an active user on Facebook. The account that I still hold today was a birthday gift from a close friend. Even still, a post on Facebook was literally the first idea that came to my mind on how to notify others about my fundraising and Everyday Hero page.

It was a Saturday morning that I created an album, "Climb 4 Kids: Everest Base Camp 2018", on my page and wrote a simple and short post with a link to my fundraising page. After I came back from my morning walk, I received notifications that I'd received a couple of donations on the fundraising page. In response to my post, some of my friends, even those in Malaysia, donated.

Along this fundraising journey, what got me excited was never the amount someone donated, as I understood from the very beginning that every dollar counted and that people were contributing what they could. What really encouraged me was the shared belief that people had in me by answering my appeal through their act of giving. From then on, I took the effort to share my training progress and, as a way to give back, I loaded photos to share the beautiful Australian landscape and bush animals that I encountered in my training with my circle of supporters. The word spread from there, as my posts were shared among my friends' circles of friends on Facebook.

I remember my elder brother's post that read: "My sister is doing something incredible that is close to her heart. Please donate generously so that she has no way to turn back". He was right. There was no way I was turning back.

Next, I was brainstorming the idea of a fundraising movie night with my immediate team members at work, but we could not work out a cost-effective plan that made sense. The cost seemed to be too high, and that would eat away the potential of donations going to UNICEF. I was also travelling a bit due to a project I was working on. Time was not on my side from the organising side of things for this movie night. So the movie idea was dropped, but with the two complimentary "Gold Class" tickets sponsored by a local cinema, I auctioned them, and that contributed nicely to the fund.

Because I could not make a movie night work, I took the suggestion from someone at work to start fundraising by selling Cadbury chocolates. I was a bit sceptical at first whether I would be able to sell them, as the minimum purchase was 12 boxes, making a total of 720 bars of chocolate that I'd have to sell. To my own surprise, my first order was sold out within two months. Not bad from what I'd initially imagined. I placed the chocolates boxes primarily at the office where I was based and at three other office locations, where I sometimes needed to go for work. The receptionists at those offices told me people loved the fundraising chocolates. Moreover, it was supporting a good cause. I also made little flags (with stickers) and cards (the size of a name card) that went with the chocolates so that people would know what those fundraising chocolates were for, and they could take a flag or card if they wished to make a donation through my fundraising page. On those flags and cards, I also included information concerning the impact their donation would make. For example, one read, "AUD $21 could provide 500 pencils to give children the vital tools to nurture learning and a prosperous future".

I also had people tell me that when they had spare coins (AUD $1 or $2 coins) and were craving chocolate, instead of going to the vending machine, they found it more meaningful to contribute to my donation box and grab a bar of chocolate from there. Some of them intentionally chose to buy from my chocolate box over buying from the shop. I was so encouraged by the results from these chocolate bar fundraising sales that I made a second order. I remember the lady who took my order commented, "Wow, you are back for your second". She was the same lady who'd helped with my first order, and I remembered asking her for tips as I had been concerned that I wouldn't be able to sell the chocolates. The second order was equally encouraging, and I even made a third (and final) order less than a month later.

Where I worked, because we had monthly morning tea meetings for the leaders to share business updates, I thought in one of those morning teas, it would be a good opportunity to do a short presentation around my fundraising appeal. When I asked, the office manager agreed. At that point, I'd just crossed the AUD $2 thousand mark (halfway to the target), and I'd just made a five-minute thank you video that I'd posted on my Facebook page and my Everyday Hero page. I started my presentation at the morning meeting with the thank you video, followed by sharing why I'd chosen to do the challenge. I have to be honest, during my preparation I was tossing between giving a "professional" speech or allowing my heart to speak authentically. In the end, I chose the latter. I wrote down key points for prompts with the bigger aim of really allowing my heart to guide my words. Afterwards, when I received feedback from people that I'd inspired them in some ways, I learnt a powerful truth: when I speak from the bottom of my heart, I can establish a real connection and touch other people's hearts.

It was very encouraging watching the level of donations increase day by day by day, so that by the target date, when the campaign ended, the final amount I raised was AUD $6,626.91. I couldn't believe it! How was that possible if not due to the joint effort from everyone? Every dollar counted! And some very precious advice that I followed through with was that I made the effort to leave a personal thank-you message to each person who donated, even the anonymous supporters. Some, even until now, I never learned who they were.

I learnt many valuable lessons from this fundraising experience. The biggest lesson learnt was that the worries I had at the very beginning were simply fear-based assumptions. The fear I felt was because I was afraid of being judged in a bad way, a fear that never played out in reality. I know this fear isn't one that only I experience. It's true for everyone, how we can let a fear—that likely won't ever play out in reality—limit our possibilities. Really, only one thing is certain—we will only know if we'll succeed as we hope to, or fail as we fear, if we try.

9.

THE "EXERCISE TYPE"

Man is what he believes.
—Anton Chekhov

My father has long been an active person. During his teen years, he completed many long-distance bicycle rides, cycling from town to town. As an adult, his work often entailed him being very active. For example, before retiring, he worked as an estate manager, looking after the operation of a palm oil plantation, a physically demanding job that required him to be on his feet and moving around a lot. Now, at the age of 72, he still goes for a walk twice a day, even when he's travelling. He's always looking out for opportunities to do walks to maintain his fitness.

Dad has always aimed to influence my brothers and me with the benefits of regular exercise. Of course, all of us, you included, already know the importance of regular exercise, but we tend to take our health and mobility for granted when we're young, and even middle-aged. Busy with our careers, families, friends, and such, it's easy for a consistent fitness practise to drop off the radar. It's such a dangerous choice. Luckily for me, I have Dad.

As mentioned, Dad has long advocated the importance of regular exercise. When my brothers and I were young, he got us into swimming. On weekends, he would drive for hours to take us to another town so that we could use the public swimming pool there. I already shared how he grew up in a small fishing town, so being comfortable and confident in the water was a priority for him and one that he wanted for his children too.

I consider swimming the first sport in my life. While I was in primary school, I joined the school's swimming club and even had the opportunity to represent my school in a swimming competition. Unfortunately, in my first—and last—swimming competition, I came in last place in my category, the breaststroke. I didn't handle it very well. I admit there were a lot of tears, and I didn't want to go back to swimming practise again after the race. Mum and Dad encouraged me to try again the following year, but we'd moved to another town and I never got involved in any school sports again.

Admittedly, I used to think that being active and exercising meant you had to be on a team and be especially talented at a sport. You know, pretty much like a professional or a very serious athlete. And as I wasn't particularly talented at any sport and certainly wasn't on any team, I thought I just wasn't the exercise type. I've had to rewire my brain and stop these false associations between being active, being talented, sports, professional athletics, and competition. I've had to activate a new way of looking at exercise, and from there, start getting fit in the way that works for me.

Being fit has nothing to do with being elite, talented, coordinated, or gifted at a sport. It's simply a matter of being active on a regular basis in order to stay healthy. For me, being active offers me an opportunity to challenge myself, to take myself to the next level. A race between myself, and only myself.

The moment I lifted the unnecessary mental barrier around exercise that I'd created and landed on this new perspective, things changed for me. Going for an evening walk was no longer a chore but a choice. It used to be Dad who'd suggest, "Let's go for a walk", and he'd need to bribe me with a delicious dinner too. After my change in mentality, it became, "Dad, are you going for a walk? Can I come?" I started to fall in love with walking, and I noticed that I felt great after every walk as well.

Don't take my word for it. Give it a try yourself. Feel the change yourself. Start with 15 minutes of walking, two or three times a week, around your neighbourhood. Once you enjoy the change, trust me, you will want to walk farther distances and/or more often. And if you are like me, exploration will begin for you too. Perhaps you'll want to walk a long trail in your area, do a multi-day hike carrying your own gear, or climb to the top of a mountain in your locale—you never know.

As you know, I've done some amazing treks in Malaysia. But there's a difference between selective training for a trek and daily exercise when you don't have a big hike or climb in mind. As you can expect, I advocate both! After I moved to Sydney, I made walking a part of my daily life. Walking and using public transport have long been my mode of travel. Also, because I was new to the country, I wanted to explore. Over a period of time, my city exploration walks expanded to coastal and bushwalks. With this said, I already had a base level of fitness and experience doing walks in the Sydney area and beyond when I started training for the trek to Everest Base Camp.

The Everest Base Camp (EBC) trek is for those willing to train. It is a physical challenge. The distance would be about 130 kilometres, 65 there and 65 on the return, done over 13 days (but some of those days are acclimatisation days, which I'll talk about shortly). We would walk on average 15 kilometres a day over three to seven hours, depending on the terrain and other factors. Typical gains in elevation would be around 300 to 400 metres each day. The fact we'd be doing all this at a high altitude meant that we'd be doing it with half the oxygen we're used to taking in, which would make everything way, way harder and slower. The adventure difficulty level is ranked a 5/5, meaning it is as difficult as it gets. From the very beginning, I understood that the fitter I was for the trek, the more I would be able to enjoy it. So, in the year before the trip, I continued my efforts to get fit and maintain it.

I drafted a training plan to prepare for the EBC trek, using online research for recommendations on where to train in the Sydney area. I committed myself to a four- to six-hour bushwalk, at least once a week, either on a Saturday or a Sunday. I bundled that with other activities—like swimming, cycling, and shorter walks—on weekdays.

Trekking at altitude is a challenging but exhilarating experience, but there are also many dangers that can lead to severe injury or even death. Therefore, from day one, starting from the information packet, I understand the importance of being well-prepared with special warm, waterproof clothing and of being very careful and cautious. As such, accompanied in the bushwalk training was my daypack, holding the very items that I would be taking with me during the actual trek, like my water bag (that held two litres of water), a waterproof coat and pants, other cold weather gear, a personal first aid kit, walking sticks, and other items like a camera, sunscreen, lip balm, hat, snacks, toilet paper. It was essential that I trained carrying this daypack in order to get myself used to walking with this weight and bulk. And because the trek participants had a guideline of six to seven kilos total for the daypack that we had to stick with, that helped a lot in determining which essentials were and were not essential. It also helped fine-tune my packing process—which items would go at the bottom and which at the top based on how easy and frequently I'd need to retrieve them; how to arrange items so that the pack was comfortable to carry, etc.

Another danger in undertaking an altitude trek that sometimes puts people off is the possibility of getting the altitude sickness. The sickness occurs because of ever-decreasing oxygen levels as we go up in altitude, especially when we're higher than 3 thousand metres above sea level. If the ascent is too fast and/or the height gain is too great, our body acclimatisation mechanism does not have the chance to work properly. From my research, I came to know that we can't train to prevent altitude sickness (gulp). The main way to prevent it was by a gradual ascent, slow and steady walking, avoidance of alcohol and other sedatives, and drinking and eating adequately. At this information, my eyes lit. "Hey, I can do that!" In fact, going slowly was certainly very appealing to me. I knew that these measures were no guarantee, but at least I could do something to try my best to prevent it. Therefore, I incorporated into my training consciously establishing a slow and steady pace. As for the elevation part, practising walking at high elevations, I knew I couldn't do much about it, especially as I was in Australia, where great elevations weren't easy to reach. I decided not to let that bother me too much and to focus on what I could do consistently.

From taking on this challenge, I realised something about myself—when I have a defined goal, it acts as a solid push factor for me to stay disciplined. I'll tear down any walls to stick to my plan to achieve the goal. I'll choose to do the thing that is right for that moment, that I know I need to do, even if I don't feel like doing it. A solid goal gives me a tremendous level of determination.

On more than one occasion, I chose to wake up as early as 3:30 am to catch a 5:00 am train so that I could arrive at the Katoomba train station around 7:00 am to start my training walk. There were no buses operating at such early hours. Meaning to say, to reach the starting point of my walk, I had to walk from the Katoomba train station and yet I chose to do that.

At other times, I showed myself my own determination when I chose to climb up the Giant Stairway, as opposed to going down it. This is how the site www.weekendnotes.com describes the famous Giant Stairway, "At 540 metres in length with 911 steps hewn from the cliff face and 32 steel staircases, the aptly named Giant Stairway drops almost three hundred metres to the floor of the mighty Jamison Valley below the Three Sisters". When I attempted the 911 steps and 32 staircases for the very first time, it was tough. Did I go back to do it again? Yes, I did! Why? Because I knew it helped to build my stamina. Plus, I knew the trek to EBC would be many times more challenging than that. I knew I needed to do the hard work now, not later.

Plus, Mother Nature rewards those who do the hard work. When I trained in the Blue Mountains, I always made sure to start as early as possible. In the early morning, you actually have higher chances of meeting native bush animals. One morning when I was about 10 to 15 minutes into my walk, I heard the sound of the lyrebirds. In case you don't know, lyrebirds are famous for their ability to mimic sounds around them, both natural and artificial (like sounds of machines). To my surprise, there was one in the bush area over to my right and another two in front, walking towards me! Lyrebirds are also famous for their feathers, especially males with their monumental tail feathers. I felt so blessed to be able to admire them at such proximity.

On another training day, I met the brushturkey for the very first time while I was having my snack. As there were no other people around, just me, the bird came close to me, and at one point I thought it was eyeing my grapes!

My other training route was from the Berowra Train Station to the Cowan Train Station. It is approximately 12.9 kilometres per way and on average took me about 4.5 hours to complete. The walk makes up one of the sections of the famous Great North Walk. It is very scenic taking you down to the Berowra Water before you walk back up the valley again. Then there is a good stretch of moderate uphills, which, again, served as very good training for me. I even bumped into the same gentlemen twice on two different days. The second time, we exchanged a brief conversation. I came to know that he was training for his upcoming holiday to Canada. I told him about my upcoming trek as well. We wished each other well in our respective adventures. If I ever see him again, I hope I can recognise him, and we can exchange stories of our adventures.

When I look back over the efforts I made to prepare myself for the EBC trek, it is very encouraging to see my own dedication. At the time, it was very encouraging when others cheered along with me and voiced that they were inspired by my dedication. It also proved to me, "If I want to do something, I can do it!" This is true for you too. All you need is the courage to first decide what you want to do. Once you set your mind to it, you will find ways to get there. Everything you experience along the journey will become your unique story. It is a legacy that you can share. And the person you become will be worth all the efforts.

In the upcoming chapters, please accompany me on a magical journey in Nepal. Through my words, I would like to inspire you to find your version of "Everest Base Camp"!

PART II.
STORIES AS ASPIRATION

10.

NEPAL—MAJESTY AND MYSTICISM

Visiting Nepal has been on my bucket list for many years. What I was never sure about was when I would be going. From the beginning, I knew setting foot in Nepal would bring me magical moments. True enough, it started the day we landed in Kathmandu.

Kathmandu, the gateway to the Himalayan mountains, is located in a vast valley where there'd once been a large lake. It is an incredible historic city with eye-catching architecture and exquisite wood carvings and metal crafts, which clearly showcase the skills of the Newar artisans, the historical inhabitants of the Kathmandu Valley and the surrounding area. Kathmandu is a place where Hinduism and Buddhism coexist in harmony, thus adding another layer of colour to the legends abounding the city. Every street has a shrine or two, and the residents make little distinction as they worship in both Hindu and Buddhist shrines.

My first impression was that Kathmandu seemed to have zealously guarded its ancient traditions and yet at the same time, seemed to take some effort to embrace modern technology. One particular example stood out for me during the city tour we did on the first day. On this tour I noticed a mobile phone retailer set up in a traditional building structure. I could also imagine that with the many visitors pouring in, Kathmandu must have seen rapid expansion. But despite the fast life common to metropolises, I must say Kathmandu's people remained friendly towards visitors. At least that was how I felt. I loved seeing their smiles even though they were apparently very impoverished people. I must admit too that the traffic overwhelmed me. Being used to the orderly manner of traffic in Sydney, with the help of traffic lights and pedestrian crossings, my heart seemed to pump more quickly when attempting to cross the busy main streets in Kathmandu. What an experience!

Retaining its ancient tradition, Kathmandu is blessed by the Living Goddess, Kumari, a young Newar girl who represents the incarnation of the powerful Goddess Taleju, the tutelary deity of the Malla Dynasty and next the Shah Dynasty, which inherited the tradition from the Malla (the Malla Dynasty was overthrown by King Prithvi Narayan Shah). The Living Goddess is worshipped with great reverence. Even the Shah kings follow the tradition of receiving blessings from her. Legend has it that King Jaya Prakash Malla, under the influence of alcohol, offended the Goddess Taleju in her human form by lusting after her while playing a game with her. She then ordered the king to make an oath that he would select a virgin girl within whom she would always reside. The tradition has since continued to this day. We visited the Kumari Ghar across Durbar Square, where the Living Goddess, Kumari, resides. However, we were not in luck to catch a glimpse of this goddess. Perhaps, the mystical will provide me with another chance to return to visit this city again.

Unfortunately, the historic areas of Kathmandu were severely damaged by the earthquake in 2015. Some of the buildings have been restored and some remain in the process of reconstruction. Thankfully, its cultural uniqueness can still be traced, and I hope it remains.

Beyond the city, from Lukla all the way to Everest Base Camp—making that move was beyond my imagination. Buckle up and get ready for the adventure I describe in the next chapter concerning this move.

11.

CRISP AIR, CLOSE CALLS

Day 1, Lukla (2,840 m) to Phakding (2,630 m)

The day's plan: a short flight to Lukla where we'd start our trek the same day, walking from Lukla, which is at 2,840 metres, to Phakding, whose elevation is actually lower at 2,630 metres. This is the traditional way to start the Everest Base Camp trek.

I came to know from Gopan, our head guide, that there was another option. Rather than flying to Lukla, you could head out from Kathmandu on a 10-hour bone-rattling bus ride to Jiri. It's between five and eight days of trekking from Jiri to reach Lukla, depending on your walking pace. The route from Jiri to EBC receives only a few visitors. While the elevation is not extremely high, the trek into Lukla from Jiri is very difficult as the trail cuts across numerous valleys, ascending and descending multiple ridgelines as it traverses the base of the Himalayas. Gopan said most trekkers consider this lower portion of the trek the more difficult one. For my very first attempt, I was more than happy to fly into Lukla.

Now, before we move further, I would like to introduce you to Gopan, our head of guide. Gopan was a Nepalese man in his 40s, with over 20 years of experience leading treks in the Himalayas. Although he had never summited Everest, the Everest Base Camp trek was one of the common treks he led, along with other routes. His wise, caring, patience shone through during the days he led our group. He was great both with us trekkers and leading his team of guides whom you will meet in the coming chapters.

He told a story about how he landed in this career path. He said that when he was a kid, he got very excited whenever there was an opportunity to meet with tourists. He did not speak good English at that young age, but that did not stop him. At that time, Nepal started to receive many visitors from Western countries. He started with the limited vocabulary he had, like "Hello" and "Good morning", and slowly as he picked up more English, he was able to communicate more and gain confidence along the way. And it was from speaking English that he got a foothold into tourism and into leading treks. I found this inspiring. Plus, from this story alone, I could see that he chose a positive approach to life, something that continued to be apparent during the days he guided us, even when things were less than ideal.

While the rest of his team would be meeting us in Lukla, Gopan met us, the group of 11 trekkers, in Kathmandu, two days prior to our flight to Lukla. He did this to ensure that if we needed anything for the trek, he could assist. For example, we might need to rent equipment, like a good quality sleeping bag. We might need assistance packing our duffel bags for the trek.

On the day of our flight, Gopan made sure we arrived at the Tribhuvan International Airport early enough that we'd have plenty of time to check in and make it to the gate for the 6:00 am flight. There was a lot of coordination going on behind the scenes to make this trek happen.

Tribhuvan International Airport was a busy airport with many trekking teams passing through it as well as Nepalese people. It was not the kind of busy that you'd expect in a big and modern international airport, but a different, localised sort of busy. It was a pretty smooth process for us. We checked in our backpacks. Our team of trekkers was allowed a combined weight for all of our gear, and thank goodness we were within the limit, phew! It was challenging to pack the correct weight for the 13-day trek. We got our boarding passes and passed the security checkpoint. We were in the waiting lounge by the gates when we took our first group photo. We were all so eager. Energised.

That's when we got news of a delay. It was foggy at the airport in Lukla, so no planes could land.

Let me give you a little background about Lukla's infamous airport. It's called the Tenzing-Hillary Airport, and Sir Edmund Hillary and the Sherpas built it in the 1960s. In case you don't know, the Sherpas are a Nepalese ethnic group. They are renowned for their climbing skills, superior strength, and endurance at high altitudes. Sherpa mountaineer Tenzing Norgay and New Zealand mountaineer Sir Edmund Hillary became the first climbers to reach the summit of Mount Everest in May 1953. Back in Sydney, when I was reading about the trek, I asked Google about this airport. That's how I learnt that it is classified as the most dangerous airport in the world for over 20 years now. (Sweat) After being there myself, I understood why. More on that shortly!

A delay, both into and out of the Lukla Airport, is a common situation. It is due to its geographical location of being surrounded by tall mountains. The weather can also make the landing and take-off dangerous. Hence, its designation as the most dangerous airport in the world. Yet, on a clear day, it will reward you with exceptional views as you head towards the airstrip.

For us, the first news of a one-hour delay was followed by a second one-hour delay. Then a third one-hour delay. Then ... yes, many delays. Because it happens that there have been times no planes can pass at all for an entire day, we were praying and hoping that wouldn't be our case.

The team showed an extreme level of understanding of the situation. We waited as patiently as we could for the updates. Gopan and Stuart, our team leader and trip doctor, showed great leadership too. They provided us with regular updates and at the same time considered alternatives.

As the hours passed the 12:00 pm mark, there was a need to make a decision. We could wait until 2:00 pm, the latest a flight could take off. However, if we didn't have the clearance to take off, we would go back to our hotel. We would then return the next day. With this option, if the weather was not on our side the following day, we would bump into the same situation again.

Stuart recommended we explore every possibility to get to Lukla as soon as possible because it had a direct impact on our acclimatisation schedule. As much as possible, we didn't want to lose any days planned for acclimatisation. You may be wondering why these acclimatisation days are so important.

As mentioned in an earlier chapter, the best way of avoiding altitude sickness whilst trekking in high altitude is to increase altitude gradually. In Nepal, a safe altitude to which most of us can accommodate ourselves immediately is between 2,700 metres to 3,000 metres. Lukla airport is located in this safe altitude range. On the day of our arrival, we definitely needed to spend the night at that high altitude. In fact, for us, the plan was to spend the night at Phakding, whose altitude was a bit lower than Lukla's. Thereafter, our trekking schedule incorporated a set climbing regime: a gain of 300 to 400 metres in altitude a day. Accordingly, every overnight stay would be at an altitude of 300 to 400 metres higher than our previous night's location. Once we'd climbed a total of approximately a thousand metres in altitude, the plan was to devote one whole day to altitude acclimatisation by staying a second night at the same altitude. On the acclimatisation day, we would be doing a little trekking, doing a day walk up to greater altitude (again between 300 and 400 metres) before returning and staying overnight at the previous night's altitude. This acclimatisation schedule would allow our body to have the opportunity to adapt to the higher altitudes, which we were not used to. And it was very important that we had these acclimatisation days in order to avoid altitude sickness.

One of the alternative options Gopan and Stuart were considering for getting us to Lukla on schedule was going by helicopter. However, that presented other challenges. A helicopter flight to Lukla carried a maximum of five people. With our numbers, plus our bags, it would mean we'd need several helicopter flights. While an aeroplane flight would take approximately 35 minutes, a helicopter flight would take approximately 50. The additional cost of a helicopter flight was also significant.

In the end, the weather cleared, and we were able to board our flight. We all gathered our backpacks and hopped into a minibus that took us to the plane. While waiting for our luggage to load into the 24-seater plane, I looked at the sky. I felt it was bluer than I had ever before noticed. A feeling of gratitude came out from me, and I couldn't thank Mother Nature enough for giving us such big help. At the same time, excitement swept over me. "This is it, the beginning of a spectacular and exciting journey!"

The landscape changed as we left the buzzing city behind. I got lost in my thoughts while admiring the bird's eye view of the mountain regions. I was videoing out the window when our plane seemed to be pulling up to a vertical angle, like it was trying to be a rocket ship to the stars. After several seconds, it levelled out again. I realised I'd been holding my breath. Actually, it seemed we all released our breaths in unison. It hadn't been just me. Everyone had gotten nervous.

I looked out the window. We were approaching the airport, as I could see an airstrip. When the plane landed, everyone cheered for the pilot.

Later on, I found out what had happened. It wasn't any stunt that our pilot was doing to add unnecessary excitement to our flight. He was trying to avoid a collision with another plane, which appeared below our plane right before our landing. I later heard that air control in the Lukla Airport might not be as efficient as at other bigger airports. Thus, there could be times the pilots would need to exercise their own judgement. Hmm. The unexpected thrills of travelling!

A cool wind brushed my face as I stepped out of the plane. I breathed the crisp air into my lungs. So exhilarating! Looking around, I gasped in shock. The airstrip was very short and at its end was a sharp drop-off. A cliff. It was easy to imagine how an exciting journey could turn into a disaster as the airstrip seemed to offer no room for error.

With Gopan leading us, we moved away from the airport and gathered at an open space next to a small shop. Our duffel bags had been brought over before us and lay nicely against the wall of the shop. Each of us reached for our own duffel bag and began the reshuffled process, shuffling items between our duffels and backpacks. We'd be carrying our backpacks, and our porters would carry our duffel bags.

Inspired Adventures, the fundraising agency that UNICEF Australia chose to partner with, looked after the in-country logistics side of the things. Inspired Adventures implemented "responsible travelling". What that meant for us was that to honour porters' rights, a porter only carried 15 kilograms max of other people's gear. Because on our trek we shared one porter per two of us, each of us could give a porter 7.5 kilos of gear to carry. To be honest, these limits assisted me in the packing process, helping me to pack only the most important items. In my backpack, I was carrying approximately five kilos. I was very grateful for the advice others gave me around going for very light-weight gear. It helped me tremendously.

After reshuffling our packs and refilling our water bags, it was time to start walking. First, we gathered in a circle. Apparently we were going to do a little ice-breaking session before we set out! We met Paawan and Binesh, our two assistant guides. And we met our lovely porters—Binod, Lahar, Madhur, Taran, Hasan, and Kanan. We took turns to introduce ourselves to our Nepalese support team, and we attempted to speak in Nepali as well. Here's what I remember saying to introduce myself, "Namastē mērō nāma Wei San hō", which translates to "Greetings, my name is Wei San".

The day's walk was to be a light and easy three-hour walk. Leaving Lukla, we set off through a pine and cedar forest along the Dudh Kosi River. Then we went downhill to the small village of Ghat and, next, on to Phakding, our destination. There was a bit of rain, but it did not bother us. Everyone's spirits were high, and we each moved at our own pace. Paawan was tasked to always walk at the front, leading the front group, and it was a rule for the entire trek that no-one would pass him. Then Binesh or Gopan would take turns, either staying with the middle group or the back group. With this arrangement, no-one got left behind. Three guides total worked well for us. Most of the time, I was with the back group, taking my own sweet time and absorbing the views.

Close to evening, we arrived at the teahouse at Phakding with some time to spare. Most treks in Nepal are "teahouse" treks, meaning every night the trekkers end up at a simple lodge with basic rooms and a meal (as opposed to setting up their own tents somewhere and carrying their own food, etc.). During the day, we also stopped at teahouses for our lunch and, if possible, for our morning and afternoon breaks. Thanks to these teahouses, we only needed to carry the minimal important gear. If these teahouses did not exist, we would need to carry the food supply for the 13-day trek as well as tents for camping. That would be a lot of weight!

While teahouses can vary slightly from region to region, the ones we visited were simple stone and wooden buildings that had a kitchen, a communal eating hall, a toilet/bathroom area, and a number of basic bedrooms that usually contained two single beds. The bedrooms either sat in the same building as the common rooms or were housed in a separate building. I must say, although the rooms were very basic, they were clean and comfortable. Good enough for me to have a good night's rest.

From the first day of the trek, I noticed that our porter team always arrived at the day's destination teahouse before us without fail. Even though they were walking with heavier weight, and they always left after us each morning, they always arrived before us at the destination teahouse. How did I know this? Our duffel bags were always waiting for us when we arrived. Of course, the porters were definitely fitter than us, and growing up in the mountain regions, I guessed that they were used to walking at such an altitude.

Another key factor that I came to know later was that they did not stop to rest at the teahouses along the way each day, as we did. They headed straight to the next accommodation. I remembered one of the days a group of people passed us, and I heard Gopan saying, "There are our boys". By the time I caught my breath and tried to locate them, they were already gone. Wow! Instead of saying we were helping them to make a living, I saw it as they were helping us to reach our destination by taking the weight off us.

After getting our duffel bags at the night's teahouse, we went to our rooms briefly and then gathered again in the common area to have dinner. The menus in the teahouses along our trek were very similar. I was first introduced to dal bhat, a Nepalese dish made up of rice and lentils, and served with vegetable curry, on this first night. It became my favourite meal along the trek. It's filling, fresh, and I could never resist the vegetables. Momos (steamed dumplings, and we'd normally go for a vegetable filling if we ordered one to share), pasta, pizza, and other rice and noodle dishes were also among the common foods on offer.

After dinner on our first night, a cake was brought out. It was Claire's birthday! We didn't know, but Stuart and Gopan had it all planned. Claire was from Sydney, and Everest Base Camp had been her dream for a very long time. However, after an accident a couple of years earlier, which resulted in various fractures in her body, Claire had thought this trek would never happen for her. She said with pure luck and no permanent damage from the accident, she was here to chase a forgotten dream and all the while fundraise for an organisation that she greatly admired. What I learnt from Claire—don't give up on your dream, for it will patiently wait for you to reactivate it again.

We stayed in the common area for a while that night, finishing the cake and talking briefly about timing for the next day.

That very first night, I had a hot shower. However, I didn't know that would be my last shower for the entire trek, at least until we returned to Kathmandu. It was not that there would be no opportunity; it was that I'd find it too cold to be out of my clothes for even a minute to shower!

12.

MOVING BEYOND THE ALTITUDE SICKNESS THRESHOLD

Day 2, Namche Bazaar (3,440 m) and Day 3, Acclimatisation Day

On day two, we walked to Namche Bazaar, where we would spend an extra day to acclimatise.

What accompanied us? A river valley, a blue pine and rhododendron forest, and many high suspension bridges! Crossing those suspension bridges was special to me. It always fascinates me the efforts that people put in to make connections possible. Especially in remote areas like this. The suspension bridges opened up the connection for us, the trekkers. They made visiting this beautiful region possible. The bridges also opened up connections between villages that sit at either side of the river and in the mountain areas. For the majority of the locals, walking is the main mode of transportation. Without these suspension bridges, I could only imagine the challenges they would face.

Following lunch, we entered the gates of Sagarmatha National Park. After a few more river crossings, before we began the steep ascent to Namche Bazaar, we crossed the famous Hillary Suspension Bridge. It was very exciting. It is one of the tallest suspension bridges in Nepal. At a height of 135 metres and decorated by many prayer flags, it stands just above the Dudh Koshi River (some call it the "white colour river"). Whether we were ready for it or not, this suspension bridge at its length of 344 metres was what we'd cross to enter Namche Bazaar. I heard the possible alternative was a tough one-hour walk. How tough was it? I wasn't sure. The idea of crossing this epic, scary bridge was more appealing to me.

Trust me, as scary it may sound and look, being so high up on the bridge was an incredible experience. I was very grateful to have been given some tips in order to enjoy the epic bridge crossing experience. Here are some of those tips: do not rush to cross the bridge, give yourself the chance to soak in the views while on the bridge and to take pictures. Allow porters, yaks, and donkeys space to traverse the bridge at their speed. Beforehand I even tried to mentally rehearse what I'd do if I met an oncoming yak or donkey caravan, but luckily I didn't encounter one.

The movie "Everest" features this bridge in one of its scenes, and I couldn't believe I was actually crossing the bridge myself. When I reached the middle of the bridge, I deliberately looked down, and from that height I must admit my heartbeat jumped a bit. I took a deep breath and brought myself back. Soon the sound of the rushing river under me took over. I soaked in the 360-degree mountain views. And at that very moment, I felt like I could hear Mother Nature whispering in my ears, "Welcome, Wei San, and enjoy your magical journey!"

Towards the end of our day's trek, the mighty Mount Everest, which the Nepalese call Sagarmatha, came into our view for the first time. Sagarmatha is derived from Nepali words "sagar", which means "sky", and "mātha", which means "head". Some translate it into "forehead of the sky". Being the highest peak on the earth, I think it explains it all. It was so moving and exhilarating to see the majestic mountain peak with my own eyes. It looked gorgeous even from the distance. I did have a quick flash of thought, "Will I think about the possibility of standing at that peak one day?" You never know. But definitely, it was not my focus at the moment. We rested and took some time to absorb the view before we continued on.

As planned, we arrived at Namche Bazaar in the late afternoon. Because we had some spare time before dinner, some of us went for a walk to explore the town.

Namche Bazaar is the staging point for expeditions to Everest. It also offers a great location to aid in the ever-important altitude acclimatisation process because it is the first place on the trek that is above the altitude sickness threshold. It is also the gateway to other higher Himalayan peaks. Gopan said the town had developed a lot and become quite colourful over the years. It all started to happen after Sir Edmund Hillary and Tenzing Norgay's successful climb to Everest's peak. Many other climbers and trekkers followed in their footsteps. I can imagine Namche Bazaar must have prospered a lot due to tourism. Despite its prosperity, the town seemed to have kept its ancient culture and heart-warming hospitality. It has simply added on another layer of colour.

I observed many things available for sale here. Ranging from Tibetan artefacts, like hand-held prayer wheels, singing bowls, bronze and gold gilt statues of Buddhist and Hindu deities, and saddle rings and bracelets, to trekking and climbing equipment from big brands like The North Face, Black Diamond, and Salomon. Everything a person needed during a trekking trip. Most of the shops, especially the smaller ones, preferred to trade in their own Nepalese Rupee, but some bigger shops accepted US Dollars. Thankfully, there were also currency exchange facilities too. Gopan reminded us that this was the last place that had this service available and that we should ensure we had sufficient cash for the remainder of our journey, as the upcoming places where we'd be stopping only accepted the Nepalese Rupee. As you can imagine, the exchange rate would be much lower than in Kathmandu.

I fell in love with the special geography of Namche Bazaar the moment I arrived. The way it sits on crescent-shaped mountain slopes (like an oval-shaped stadium, only not a full oval) I found quite unique. When you move to the higher section of the village, it offers stunning views of the mountains across the valley.

Namche Bazaar is a major trading centre of the Khumbu region. It invites traders from Tibet and Sherpas from neighbouring villages to gather to trade. It has hotels, teahouses, lodges, restaurants, pubs, cyber cafes, and German bakeries. I was quite amazed by the fact that cafes and German bakeries were common, as that was not something I was expecting. And they were not only in Namche Bazaar but also in some smaller towns and villages that we stopped in. At first, I figured it was due to the fact there were so many Westerners trekkers coming through. But still, why German bakeries? It turned out, there are stories that explain.

I was told that in the past, there was a German trekker who fell in love with Nepal after his first trekking trip. He continued to return. A baker himself, he started to share his baking recipes with the locals. His recipes were passed around, and that's how German bakeries spread in the region. Some people may ask, "How true is this story?" For me, I am fascinated by a simple act of generosity that turned into such a great economic benefit to the locals, as the bakeries offer them a different source of income.

Here's another version of the story behind the German bakeries—Nepal suffered after the earthquake in 2015. Germany was among the many countries that sent help to rebuild Nepal. For example, in the Khumbu region, a hospital was under construction. It was a joint project between Nepal and Germany. And it's this collaboration, according to this version of the story, that led to the boom of German bakeries in the region.

Just to make another comment on these German bakeries, while I enjoyed the Nepalese food, especially the vegetarian options, once the journey got tougher, being able to taste a German baked good—a chocolate croissant, a raspberry tart—was quite a reward to keep me going. So I was glad the German bakeries were there.

How do the Nepalese in the mountain region earn a living? Generally, men become porters or guides. Porters don't only carry tourists trekking equipment. Seeing as villages are located on steep trails up in mountains, so they aren't accessible by vehicle, most porters actually transport goods by foot from village to village, town to town. It is a physically demanding job. About females and portering: I observed some Nepalese women along our path carrying lighter items on their backs. However, I wasn't sure if it was paid light-portering work or if they were doing the carrying for other reasons.

What about those who can't do this carrying? What do they do for work? The government put in initiatives to help locals build teahouses, lodges, small shops, and cafes, like the German bakeries. And I noticed that among these businesses, there wasn't a lack of women business owners. Along our trek, we visited at least two teahouses where females seemed to be the owners. These small businesses support the increasing numbers of trekkers to the region and that creates job opportunities. Statistics show that, on average, the amount spent by one tourist a day is able to support the daily expenses of nine Nepalese families. Crazy, right?

While some adventurous hikers or else those on a tight budget don't hire guides or porters, I recommend it. Or, at the minimum, a guide. For one, their fee is not such a great amount for those of us coming from the developed world, but it means so much to them. I found the hospitality from the guides to be extraordinary. They didn't just show us a thing or two, but many interesting things that we wouldn't have discovered for ourselves. They are not only your guides and porters, but they are also like friends, and they take care of you. Because of the high altitude, the trekking is very taxing on the body and can even be dangerous if not done properly, and the guides have experience helping people cope with this. That came from my personal experience, as you'll read in the coming chapters.

The next day, our acclimatisation day, we hiked to a higher altitude in the morning to aid in our acclimatisation. Along the way, we had a short visit to the Sagarmatha National Park Museum. Entry to the museum was free (and donations were certainly welcome), and it had good exhibitions about the people, culture, geology, and the history of the region.

Outside the museum, there were great views of Lhotse (it means "South Peak" in Tibetan and is the fourth highest mountain in the world at 8,516 metres) and across the valley to Ama Dablam whose main peak stands at 6,812 metres and whose lower western peak is at 6,170 metres. I liked how this mountain got its name. Ama Dablam means "mother's necklace". The long ridges on each side of the mountain were like the arm of a mother (ama) protecting her child. Then "dablam", the word for the traditional double-pendant necklace containing pictures of the gods that Sherpa women wear, came into the picture because of the hanging glacier.

What I found very exciting was the statue of Tenzing Norgay with Everest in the background. This was also located just outside the museum. Aside from the group photos that we took, I had a couple of photos there just by myself. Who knows, these photos may one day inspire me to climb to Everest's summit!

The afternoon was free for us, so I took a leisurely walk, had a chocolate croissant, and returned to the room with Heidi, who was my great companion along this great journey.

Heidi had a dream of making a difference in the world. A long-time supporter of UNICEF Australia, Heidi was deeply inspired by the work they do. She believed that the more people know about UNICEF Australia, the greater the organisation's impact. By way of supporting the organisation, she decided to take on this challenge and to fundraise for UNICEF Australia. A dream will always remain a dream if we do not act upon it, and Heidi acted as a great example of the grandeur of realising a long-held dream.

For the trek, I also brought with me an Irish tin whistle. It was light enough to carry and would provide me the musical outlet I cherish. I hoped it could serve as fun entertainment to others too.

Heidi listened to me play. I, too, was enjoying hearing the music ringing in the air in such a peaceful environment. However, I noticed that my breathing while playing was getting difficult. I figured that this only made sense, considering the altitude. It seemed that I ignored the first warning sign.

13.

COULD THIS BE THE END?

Day 4, Tengboche (3,860 m)

Fog greeted us as we started the day's trekking. We left Namche Bazaar by following a trail high above the Dudh Kosi River. We were climbing towards the National Park Headquarters. Gopan explained that the Dudh Kosi River originated from the high upper areas of Mount Everest. The melted snow and glacier contributed a significant part of the streamflow. It began east of Gokyo Lakes and flowed south to Namche Bazaar. Then continuing south, the river exited Sagarmatha National Park. Then passed to the west of Lukla.

After explaining, he asked, "Does anyone want to have a quick bath in the river?"

You need a huge amount of courage to even place a foot into its cold water. So, we all gave it a pass!

Closer to our lunch stop, we met a yak convoy. It was my first yak encounter, a long-haired creature I had long wanted to meet. A yak is a kind of robust cattle-like animal with a bulky frame, short but thick legs, and rounded cloven hooves. They have small ears and wide foreheads with horns too. Their most distinctive feature is an extremely dense, shaggy, long coat of hair that hangs below their belly and makes you want to give them a hug (at least, that's what I wanted to do). Yaks are actually the mammals that live at the highest altitudes in the world and can climb up as high as about 6,000 metres. Due to the nature of their body mechanisms, they are well-adapted to the cold but will begin to suffer from heat exhaustion if temperatures go above 15 degrees Celsius. No wonder you only see them in higher altitudes.

Yaks are very useful Himalayan animals. They carry goods (loads up to 100 kilos), plough fields, and provide meat, milk, butter, wool for clothing, and even dung for fuel (you will read my discovery of this fact in chapter 17). Not only that, their bones are used to make various instruments. Their hair is used to make rope, sacks, and tents. In fact, we were told even their horns are used as ornaments in doorways and rooftops.

The black yak convoy that we met seemed to be "off work" as they had no loads on their backs. As we gave way for them to pass, I secretly gave one of them a gentle touch. It felt really comfy, even at that light touch!

Then we stopped for lunch. Dal bhat, the meal I mentioned already, was the typical go-to meal for many of us in the trekking group. Even for the locals, they will eat it two or even three times per day. Some of the days, I noticed myself choosing dal bhat for lunch and then again for dinner. Of course, there are many other food options. I think everyone in our group had a silent agreement not to eat heavy lunches. One thing though, we were advised that it was best to avoid meat as all the meat was flown into Lukla and then carried by porter or yak up to the villages at higher altitudes, so it was likely the meat had been out of a refrigerated environment for some time. Especially the higher we went.

For this lunch, I opted for delicious eggs and fried rice. While the cost of meals was covered in the travel package, any drinks we got were at our own expense. You could have tea, coffee, or warm water. Sometimes, the team ordered a pot of ginger-lemon-honey tea to share. I personally liked it because it not only kept me warm, it helped soothe my throat, which was scratchy, especially as we moved higher and into ever-drier air. Depending on how many people were sharing the tea, you got to choose from a small, medium, or big pot. Stuart got the nickname "Big Pot" when we stopped at the very first teahouse. Both he and I wanted the ginger-lemon-honey tea, so we thought to order a pot to share. Without prior knowledge of "how big is the size of a big pot?", he ordered one, thinking that the two of us could easily finish it. We ended up getting help from four others with everyone having two cups apiece. That one pot only cost 400 Nepalese Rupees, or about AUD $5.

From our lunch spot, I could see the route to Tengboche snaking up the mountain ahead. Yes, a big hill was coming up, but I was ready. Excited.

Right after lunch, I was getting myself prepared as usual when sudden dizziness hit me. It slammed me, but then disappeared in a split second. "What just happened?" I asked myself. I thought I should walk even more slowly. Again, I ignored the second warning sign, falsely thinking maybe it was an effect from the lunch.

As I slowly climbed uphill, I found myself struggling. We were only about a quarter into the climb, and I was perplexed. "During my training, I did slopes steeper than this. Why am I struggling with this one?"

It was my brain that kept my body going. Asking, begging the body not to give up. I felt my feet getting heavier and heavier. It was like my feet were trying to carry all my body weight. Trying and progressively failing. I slowed down a lot.

Gopan, who was following behind me, asked, "Are you okay?"

I admitted that I was struggling.

We took a break from there. Stuart came to check on me too. They offered to carry my backpack for me, to lighten the weight. I appreciated their offer, and frankly, I was thankful that I was willing to accept help. I was glad that my ego did not take over and affect my judgement.

I acknowledged the struggles my body was having, but I was not willing to give up. My brain was still in charge and decided that accepting help was a better option if I wanted to continue the trek. Other team members noticed my struggles and came to check on me too. Their words of encouragement were fuel to keep me going.

Once we continued on, my situation did not improve. In fact, it was getting worse. I tried not to take a long break and took short breaks instead. I remembered repeating these sentences in my brain, over and over again, "We can do this. One step at a time. Every step we move forward will take us one step closer to the destination".

Gopan followed behind me, with my backpack, and watched my steps. It was very comforting to have him by my side.

I kept on going and refused to give up. However, today's walk felt very long. Repeatedly, I tried my best to push the haphazard negative thoughts from my mind and maintain a laser focus: "Get to the next village, so I can rest". I knew that any negativity in my thoughts would eat away and destroy the scarce positivity I had remaining and would do so at a very fast rate. I had no energy to observe my surroundings, nor was I enjoying the views.

I was in my zone, battling pain in effort to maintain focus and keep walking, one step at a time, when Gopan's voice broke me away from it, "We are there!"

I looked up, and a village and a grand monastery appeared in front of me. Tengboche. I felt so relieved. Like a heavy rock was lifted from my shoulders. My spirit lifted just a bit.

Tengboche Gompa, or monastery, is one of the most famous Buddhist monasteries in Nepal. It has a residing Rinpoche, a religious teacher held in high regard among Tibetan Buddhists, who blesses pilgrims, mountaineers, and travellers passing through. It is the religious and cultural centre of the Khumbu region. With Mount Ama Dablam as its unrivalled backdrop, the monastery receives many visitors all year long. Since its founding in 1912, the monastery has been destroyed and rebuilt twice as a result of earthquakes and fire.

Because it lies on the popular trek route to the Everest region, Tengboche has many rest houses and numerous lodges to cater to visitors. After a quick tour of the monastery, we headed towards our lodge.

Tengboche offers mind-numbing views. Located on a hill at the junction of the Dudh Kosi and the Imja Khola Rivers, it is surrounded with a stunning panoramic view of Everest, Lhotse, and Ama Dablam. But even with such great views, I was worn-out. All I wanted was to rest. Although I wasn't keen on any food at the time, I knew I could not allow myself to skip any meals. The moment we stopped eating, we stopped replenishing our body. We then stopped generating the energy needed to carry on. No more trekking.

During the entire journey thus far, I'd noticed changes in my appetite. From a full plate of rice, to a little less, to a little more less. The good thing was, I was still eating even though the amount got smaller and smaller. At the beginning of the trek, I could go for a full breakfast with two eggs, baked beans, and toast. At the very end of the trek, two eggs were all I could manage.

I gulped down the tomato noodle soup that I ordered for my dinner that night and went straight to bed. In the middle of the night I woke up, feeling feverish. I drank as much water as I could. Negative thoughts crept in: "Am I able to continue? Does this mean this is the end for me?"

I refused to give up. At the same time, I was struggling about whether I should go see Stuart. It was the middle of the night.

From the very beginning, Stuart made himself clear. If we were unwell and had any concern about continuing on, we were free to see him. As a doctor in a hospital emergency department, he was trained to handle emergency situations. Still, I wasn't sure if I should be knocking on his door at such a late hour. Could I wait until the next morning?

After an hour that felt like many hours, my instinct told me I shouldn't wait. I got out of my sleeping bag and went to knock on his door.

Stuart answered the door, and, wow, I respected his commitment to being on standby for us. I told him about my situation. He reckoned most likely I'd started to develop altitude sickness. As slow as I was going, I still couldn't seem to avoid it. My body had given me an official warning.

My fingers were very cold that night, so Stuart could not take the oxygen-level reading in my blood with his equipment. But, he was positive that I was not in a severe situation yet. Otherwise, I would not be able to respond to his questions.

I felt a little relieved. He gave me Panadol and half a dose of an altitude sickness pill. The Panadol was to help with my fever, and the altitude sickness pill was to give my body's acclimatisation mechanism a helping hand. We were going to assess my situation again in the morning.

I remembered crawling back into my sleeping bag and having a little conversation with myself. I asked myself to be rational. If I needed to turn back, I asked myself to please listen to any recommendation about it and do so. And if my altitude sickness developed further, there was no better way to battle it than going down to lower altitudes as quickly as possible.

The words of my loved ones before my departure kept playing in my ears:

A Loved One: Listen to yourself. At any point in time, if you are feeling uncomfortable or unwell, please don't push through. You can always return and do it another time.

A Loved One: I read an article about the amount of rubbish left at Everest. San, think about it, it is such a sacred place. Do you want to "litter" yourself [i.e., die there. There are the frozen dead bodies of trekkers who didn't make it near Everest's summit] at such a prestigious place? So, please make sure you come home safely.

A Loved One: I know it's been a year of hard work going through the training, so giving up will be a very hard decision to make. But, if you ignore the warnings and the situation turns ugly, you may lead yourself into an even more difficult situation.

Then I talked to myself again, saying, "I know you do not want to disappoint the people who supported you through this journey. If they were in front of you right now, what would they say to you? If they had to choose between the option of having you complete the challenge or having you get home safely, I'm sure you know the answer".

"What if I am afraid to fail myself?"

"What's there to be afraid of? The judgement of failure? No! Knowing when to give up is an act of courage. You are giving yourself a second chance to be more prepared and ready".

My mind was crystal clear. I felt weary again and soon fell into my sleep.

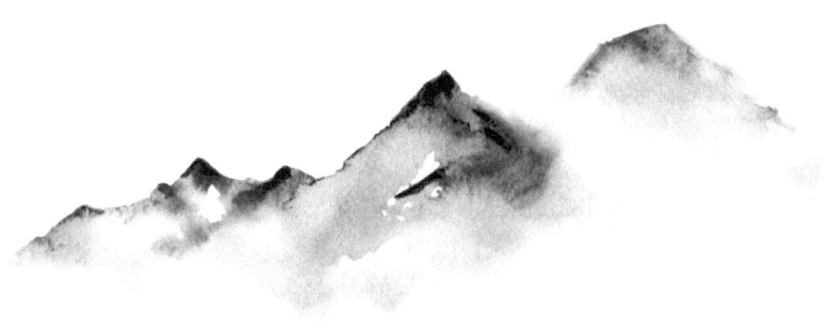

14.

RETURNING WITH A HEART OF GRATITUDE

Day 5, Dingboche (4,410 m) and Day 6, Acclimatisation Day

At the sound of the alarm, I opened my eyes and instinctively touched my forehead. The heat has gone. I sat up excitedly. The medication worked! I wasn't back at my full energy level, but I was feeling much better.

After I got changed, I headed down to meet the others for breakfast. The team asked how I was feeling and noted that I looked much better.

I answered with the cheeky words, "I'm b-a-a-a-a-a-ck!"

Everyone burst into laughter. Stuart was particularly relieved. Later on, he admitted that he'd been a bit worried that I might not be able to pull through. That I hadn't looked well that previous day and I'd seemed to be getting worse even while at dinner. When I'd knocked at his door in the middle of the night, his worry had grown.

But because my consciousness had remained clear, that had been a positive sign. He'd hoped the medication would work, and it had.

Deep down from my heart, I was thankful we had Stuart with us. I was grateful to have a wonderful team who stood by me while I was struggling. The feeling of gratitude continues to warm my heart even now when I reflect back on the experience.

After breakfast, I walked outside to have a look at the surroundings. Wow, it felt so good to be able to get absorbed in the astonishing view in front of me again.

As we headed towards an even higher altitude, I asked myself to go at my own pace. I was well aware that I wouldn't be at my full energy and that I needed more space to continue on. I was motivated by the good turn of events and my ability to react to the setback. The fact that I was still able to continue made me appreciate the journey even more. This proved to me another powerful lesson—in every situation, it's your attitude that determines the outcome.

Coming out from a bad day, my gratitude asked me not to let my attention rest on the difficulties of the day. The views around me helped to keep my spirit high.

When Gopan shared one of his views, he ended up increasing my enjoyment of this journey to an even higher level. He explained that he didn't regard any treks that he takes or any mountain peaks that he reaches as "conquering". He sees each one simply as a golden opportunity that Mother Nature offers to share with us. "Be kind, be appreciative, and Mother Nature will show us more". I love that.

So, Mother Nature offered me a spectacular view of Mount Ama Dablam as we ascended that day. I looked not only with my eyes but also with my heart. As I reflect on the journey, it began with me seeing this entire event as a challenge that I would like to complete. Everest Base Camp as a destination that I would like to conquer. Then, it transformed. It taught me something deeper. It was the next level of appreciation. It resulted in me allowing the experience to appear before me as if it were a person—the peak of Mount Ama Dablam felt like a mother guiding her child when I saw it right in front of me. As we trekked along, the sun gave me a warm coat while the cold wind embraced me. The sound of the river's flow felt like a conversation. The mountain valley opened up every doorway under the blue sky and invited me to explore every corner of its home. Even the trails seemed to be saying to me, "Go on, San, we will be with you every step".

The surroundings opened up my thinking space. My worldview. My notion of reality and living in the world. It was amazing! Despite the physical challenge that awaited, the journey became even more pleasant.

We arrived at Dingboche as planned and would spend two nights there, with the next day there being a day to aid our acclimatisation. I came to learn that the village never used to have a settlement. Over time, though, it became one of the acclimatisation points for both trekkers and climbers of Mount Everest (8,848 metres), Ama Dablam (6,812 metres), Lobuche (6,119 metres) and Imja Tse (6,160 metres), also known as Island Peak. It is the best place to continue to see the sun and avoid the icy air coming from the Khumbu region. A community developed there because of tourism. There were lodges, teahouses for tourists, and German bakeries. All the supplies in the village were carried there by porters, yaks, or helicopters.

Heidi and I woke up the next morning and saw that frozen ice had gathered on our room window. The temperature had to be low out there. I further confirmed this when there was no running water to fill up my brushing cup. The water had frozen along with the piping system!

The low temperature did not stop our acclimatisation hike for the day. We made a good acclimatisation day by hiking to the top of Nangkartshang Peak at an altitude of 5,083 metres. It took us about three hours to reach the top. It rewarded us with a view of the exquisite mountains of Mount Tawache, Ama Dablam, Island Peak, and Lhotse. We even got to see an eagle soaring in the blue sky above us.

When the sun shone on me, it was such a soothing and comfortable feeling. Overlooking the village from up high, the views that came through my eyes were sensational. As I was indulging in the moment, Gopan, Paawan, and Binesh informed us that we needed to head down immediately as they could see the clouds gathering above us. How quickly the weather could change in the mountain area. It was sunshine the minutes before and suddenly cloudy.

After lunch, I went with a few others to a German bakery across from our lodge. I had a chocolate croissant again (yum!) before returning to the room for a nap. The plan was to have a short nap, but by the time Binesh came knocking on the door, it was already dinner time. Heidi had been napping too. Wow! We were tired. Or too comfortable in our warm and cosy sleeping bags. Oops!

15.

MOMENTS OF REALISATION

Day 7, Thugla (4,620 m) and Day 8, Lobuche (4,920 m)

As the air became thinner, I continued to move slowly on today's climb to Thugla. Since day one, I kept reminding myself that this was not a race against anyone. I was free to take the pace that suited me best. To be honest, the reminder was embedded so deeply in my mind that it had become natural. An integral part of me and my approach to the trek as a whole. And this leads me to point out another important life lesson: while I was trekking, I wasn't putting my focus on things like whether I was the last in the group or not. I wasn't bothered by the fact I was not at the speed of the average trekker. My priority was crystal clear to me: I wanted to inspire others by sharing this wonderful experience, sharing what I saw and discovered, and how I felt regarding the entire journey. How I reached the Everest Base Camp was just one part; how I got back was another part. My biggest aim was around returning home to be able to tell the story in order to inspire others to follow their dreams. This bigger purpose drove every decision.

Now and then during the trek, I took the time to reflect on my life. Guess what I learned? I had not yet embedded this important life lesson very deeply into my daily life. How many times had I given in to others' expectations? When was the last time I'd reviewed the rushed pace of my life? Was I still following the path to my life's greatest priority—to spread positivity, touching people's lives, giving and sharing more—or had I drifted away from that and allowed the daily routines and norms to overrule me?

Dr. Wayne Dyer once observed: "If you are going to follow your bliss and make a difference in the world, you will soon learn that you can't follow the herd".

I knew the difference between the mountain-me and the daily-me. At the mountain, I poured all my energy and attention to "respond" to my one-and-only priority and that determined all my reactions. I chose to do hard things because they were the right things to do. The daily-me seemed to easily fall into the trap of doing easy or convenient things because, after a day of busy life, after trying to react to every single thing, I just wanted a break. Day in, day out, when you are just reacting, it's even harder to give your bigger purpose (especially when you can't see it yet) the response or attention it requires to grow stronger.

It actually feels great when you find out areas that can be improved in your life because once you acknowledge it, you are best positioned to make changes. There is a lot of work that I needed to do to keep on track. But at least, I had a direction to follow. Writing this book for you is part of my effort in responding to my bigger purpose.

It didn't take long to ascend to Thugla. It took approximately three hours. We started with a climb uphill. I appreciated having the walking poles as they helped to take quite a lot of pressure off my knees. They did not make the trekking easy, but they definitely made it easier.

Since the night at Tengboche, I had to continue taking the altitude sickness pill twice a day: half a dose in the morning and half a dose at night. I was not sure what would happen if I didn't, and I was not willing to take the risk as we moved higher and higher. It felt like my body acclimatisation mechanism was no longer able to cope on its own, so partnering with the medication helped to keep the mechanism running.

Prior to the actual trek, I learned of mixed opinions about the effect of the altitude sickness pill. Apparently different people can have different reactions from it. Some respond to it well; some don't. Some people were even able to use it as a preventive measure where they started taking the pill before the sickness occurred as a way to better prevent it from happening. Once I started taking it, I'm thankful to report that the only noticeable side effect was it dehydrated me a lot. I had to consume even more water, about double the usual amount. The further effect of increased water consumption was more frequent "nature calls". Now, there is good and bad news in terms of these frequent "nature calls". The bad news is there were no toilet facilities available, especially when in the middle of the trek. The good news is that Gopan knew the appropriate spots for "nature calls": behind a big bush, a big tree, or a big rock, depending on which part of the trek we were on. At first, it felt a bit awkward, especially as a female. But since there was no other option, I asked myself to get used to it. So, in this way I was able to have another unique experience or rather, several such unique experiences a day!

Despite the uphill, I was able to admire the incredible views of the surrounding landscapes and mountains. And the good thing was after the initial climb uphill, the walk became physically less strenuous in comparison. Also, I was able to take the opportunity to catch a close photo with a yak. Too bad that it couldn't sign an autograph for me. After my short moment with the yak, we left it behind to eat its grass peacefully.

We continued on with our journey and around lunchtime, we crossed the Dudh Kosi River and arrived at Thugla on the other side. The sight of the raging river against the melting Khumbu Glacier was incredible. Dudh Kosi means "milk river" in the Nepali language. The melting snow and glacier from the high altitude areas of Mount Everest contributes a significant portion to the powerful streamflow to create distinct frothy and white effects as the water runs downward, so that's how it got its name. I can imagine how strong the current must be under that river as I saw big stones getting moved around in the river itself, and we could barely hear each other during the river crossing.

We had the whole afternoon to rest or explore the village, and as we'd spotted another German bakery, you better believe I was going to spend my time there! With some of the others in my group, I spent the afternoon there, savouring a raspberry tart this time.

I'll admit to you, I frequently found myself wondering, "Am I truly on my way to Everest Base Camp? Is this for real?" It seemed so unreal, sometimes.

Right before dinnertime, we got to witness the sunset. It felt different although it was the same sun in our same solar system. I believed the key was my being very present to it. We were not in the buzzing city area, and there was nearly nothing that I could allow myself to get distracted with. At that moment, inside me, there was a sense of peacefulness and an intense level of appreciation. I felt so blessed to be able to get so close to Mother Nature. We watched the sun set slowly behind the distant mountains until darkness took over the yellowish sky. It was a resplendent sunset, witnessed from a special place.

A 300-metre ascent awaited us the next morning. It took us about an hour to do the ascent and reach the Thugla Pass at about 4,820 metres. At this pass, you could find more than a hundred small and large memorials built for mountaineers and Sherpas who'd died on Everest, Lhotse, and other nearby mountain expeditions. The memorials were made with staggering stones and rocks, and assembled in mound-like shapes, like that of stupas. There were prayers flags tied onto the bigger memorials. The memorials were set up by family members and well-wishers in memory of those who'd lost their lives in pursuit of their mountain dreams. It was a place where you could get emotional. I will never forget one of the prayers written on one of the memorials: "Go to sleep forever in the Everest". Lives may have passed, but the spirit remains vibrant.

It served as a reminder to me, a reminder to be sensible at all times while pursuing a great dream like this that involved risk. Every decision I made could lead to a different outcome, which wouldn't only impact me, but also my loved ones and the people around me, and, of course, that included everyone I was walking with as well.

From Thugla pass, it was a nice one-hour walk to Lobuche, where we stopped for another night. That one hour was probably among the many hours when I was truly walking at the speed of a turtle (just to provide you some perspective). Never before in my life had I walked that slowly. It sounds silly now, but it was necessary for me. As you'll recall, I likely ignored the initial light warnings twice before getting that heavier signal that my body's acclimatisation mechanism wasn't coping well. Would I have been better off if I'd understood the earlier warnings? I can't be sure, but the big warning was certainly a valuable experience for me. I would like to think that at least I was able to be watchful if a similar situation started happening again or I would be more mindful if my body reaction changed yet again.

Most importantly, I was actively responding. For example, I would keep sipping water even when I wasn't thirsty simply to keep my body hydrated. I actively adjusted my pace and took more frequent short breaks when I needed to. In short, I had another level of motivation to look after myself so that I could bring myself closer to the Everest Base Camp with every step I'd take.

Lobuche is a fairly small settlement. It lies near the foot of the Khumbu Glacier, approximately 8.5 kilometres southwest of Everest Base Camp. It gets busier in April (compared to other months when it only gets visited by trekkers like us) as hundreds of porters and Sherpas from the region pass through on their way to Everest Base Camp. They move supplies, some with the aid of yaks, for various climbers and expeditions, in preparation for the Everest spring climbing season in May. We actually trekked on the same route to Everest Base Camp that the mountaineers who attempt the Everest summit climb take. While the plan for us was to turn back the same day we reached EBC, the summiters would establish their camps, acclimatise, and rest at EBC for about a month, before commencing their summit climb. As we were trekking in November, we were fortunate to avoid the crowdedness and got to experience a serene quiet instead.

The lodging options available at Lobuche used to be quite primitive, consisting of stone huts with shared bunk dormitories. In recent years, additions of more modern facilities and amenities were built, including seven lodges that provided approximately 200 rooms with twin beds in each. We stayed at a lodge like that.

After lunch, a few of us stayed back at the teahouses and a few went on to visit the nearby glacier lake. I was tempted to follow but decided to rest instead. Sometimes, you've got to make a decision that feels right at the time. Plus, the following day was our excursion to Everest Base Camp, an expected eight-hour walk.

16.

THE FINAL TEST

Day 9, Gorak Shep (5,180 m) and Excursion
to Everest Base Camp (5,364 m)

We started off earlier than usual—before sunrise—with the aim of arriving at Gorak Shep in time for the lunch break. After that, we'd continue on to Everest Base Camp and return to Gorak Shep the same day. As you can see, it was to be quite a long day and the day we'd long been anticipating!

About 15 minutes into our early-morning walk, I was trying to get a sip of water from my water bag, but I could not. "Hmm, the tube must not be connected. Let me fix this", I was thinking, but when I checked it out, I saw that the liquid water from the bag had frozen when it was pulled into the tube on its way to my mouth. So when I tell you that I felt my fingers and feet getting frozen, I hope you realise that I'm being close to literal! By the way, thank goodness Gopan was near me. He carried extra bottles of water and offered me one.

I was aching for sunlight to warm me up, so when the sun rose, I was overcome with appreciation. My spirit lifted, and I was able to notice the surroundings again. From Lobuche, we followed a broad trail parallel to the Khumbu Glacier. As the path wound over the rocky moraine towards the settlement of Gorak Shep, we followed it upwards, trekking amongst the glaciers of the world's highest peaks. It felt like a fantasy, and even friends who viewed my photos commented, "Those views look unreal, surely you used Photoshop? Nah, I know you didn't, but seriously—wow". And I wasn't even using any sophisticated camera.

When we reached Gorak Shep, on time for our early lunch, we came upon quite a crowd there. It appeared that we were not the only group headed to Everest Base Camp that afternoon.

As usual, the porter team had arrived before us with our gear. Even though we would be staying in Gorak Shep for the night, thus the porters had completed their mission, Gopan asked some of them to go with us to Everest Base Camp and back to assist those of us who needed extra help. I was one of those whom they assisted. Without prior arrangement, Binesh's younger brother Binod (wow, they sure looked alike) took my backpack and carried it for me, so I could do the final walk without the extra weight. I still cannot express enough thanks for his help.

Without that weight, I was able to pour all my energy into reaching base camp. The journey was tough—my energy bank had never reached full bars since I'd gotten unwell at Tengboche, as I'd not been able to replenish the energy back into the bank. This was true even with good sleep, consistent meals, plenty of water, and the aid of the altitude sickness pills.

The morning section from Lobuche to Gorak Shep had actually zapped quite a bit of my reserve. Heading towards higher altitudes and the cold weather added to the challenge—but it was easier compared to the section a few days earlier when I'd been distinctly unwell. So, I went slowly as usual. I didn't allow myself to think about anything too far ahead and focused on the step in front of me. Another step. And another step. I had a rough vision of the surroundings, but I was focused on a kind of mantra: "Another step ... another step ...".

Hours passed without me noticing. Then someone gave me a pat on my shoulder. It was Binesh. Not far from where we were, I saw groups of people gathered and many flags flying in the wind.

"Almost there. That's the Everest Base Camp!" Binesh told me, pointing.

I was the last in our group to reach base camp. The wind was strong. I received big hugs from the team. Believe me, at that moment, I had tears rolling from my eyes. For a couple of seconds, I could not believe I'd made it!

So many times I had imagined myself standing at Everest Base Camp, yet none of them matched reality. Particularly the moment we were to take a group photo with our UNICEF t-shirts on. There was no way I would take any layer off, not in such cold weather, so I decided to wear the UNICEF t-shirt over my other clothes. Thus, I turned myself into a blue puffy "Michelin Man". My puffy appearance gave many on my team a good laugh.

Now, there had been a different picture in my mind around how Everest Base Camp would look. I expected there to be many tents set up to house different facilities, sleeping places, a kitchen, emergency access, an internet facility, even helipads, etc. Of course, I'd forgotten that it is only during climbing season that a temporary, thin-air, pop-up city is established at the base camp. At the end of every expedition, everything is dismantled and transported down for safe storage. Nowadays, many operators choose to rent a space in nearby villages for storage to avoid the long journey back to Kathmandu. Not a bad option, especially as it probably provides another source of income for the villagers who own the storage spaces.

When I stood at the foot of the Khumbu Glacier that day, surrounded by mountain peaks, it was a bare Everest Base Camp that appeared in front of me. I felt so proud to be a part of the whole effort—the fundraising, training, and trek itself. I was overjoyed to make some kind of contribution to the programs run by UNICEF Australia. Furthermore, as I stood at the spot where probably many,

many elite mountaineers had stood before me, my mind was filled with the images of courageous men and women who'd prepared to make a successful ascent (hopefully) of the world's highest peak. That inspired me.

I was told that climbers who attempt the peak of Everest do not spend the majority of their time climbing the mountain. It's actually spent resting, acclimatising, and preparing. This is so similar to our daily life in that the person we become through the preparation and journeying—as opposed to the destination—is pivotal, is what matters most, and our dream is our trigger point! How blessed I was to be able to experience this adventure, even with the fear, uncertainty, and hardship that came along with it.

And not to forget, without the phenomenal support crews, summiting Everest would be way, way harder! So, I thought about the layers and layers of great support I'd received in my own adventure. From the trekking team members who were with me on this adventure. My cheer squads back home. My family and friends who had given me huge courage to complete this quest. I knew from day one—really, night one, about a year earlier when I'd received that email invitation—that this would not be a quest that I could achieve on my own. Not the fundraising, not the training, and certainly not the trek itself. But it was easier and possible simply because of the fantastic people who were cheering along with me. The people whom I'd met, connected with, and some of whom I'd become real friends with—they are precious.

Yes, I'd finally made it. But … the journey had not ended—time to go back. I bid farewell to the base camp and readied myself for the return.

I already tried to prepare myself in remembering that the journey back could be even harder simply because it could be easy to underestimate it. Think about it—what you've been envisioning, planning for, training for, and practising for over a year—finally you reach it. Excellent! Your mind is occupied by peak emotions. That victory feeling could take over to where you don't prepare your spirit, mind, and body for the walk back. Just because it is walking back doesn't mean it's a breeze and it's not important and it doesn't count. It's still part of the journey. It's still very demanding. And it's still an incredible gift. To not acknowledge it, to rush it, to underestimate—that's a mistake.

I wouldn't let that happen. I'd gone through the toughest bit of the journey. I'd reached my destination, and yet I hadn't completed the journey. From that point, I had a new destination to aim for. Home. As I already mentioned, it was very important to me to celebrate and share this unique experience with everyone back home. I wanted to have the opportunity to inspire others. I wanted to decide on more big dreams—and pursue them. I wanted to thank people. So, I had better pay attention and focus.

Our journey back to Gorak Shep went smoothly. That is, until the last hour. In the last hour, my body became incredibly weary to where each step was a battle. No, this wasn't altitude sickness, it was simply my own physical and mental battle due to already having trekked that day for about seven hours. Added to that, I'd run out of the water! When this happened, there were only 30 minutes left to reach Gorak Shep. Normally, that amount of time without water would have been manageable, but this time, it felt impossible. I knew it could even be dangerous. At the same time, I had no other choice. I had to keep going. Evening was approaching.

Because I'd gotten deliriously exhausted, my brain wasn't functioning normally, so it hadn't occurred to me immediately that I could ask Binesh or Binod if they had some water I could drink. Seriously, that's how depleted I'd become.

Binesh was the one who figured out what was happening to me. He realised I'd run out of water. How did he know? Because my water bag was in my backpack, and he was carrying it for me. So every time I'd needed a sip of water, he would need to stop with me. He realised that the frequent water stops we'd been making for the past few hours had ceased.

He offered water from his water bottle to me. I was very reluctant to take it, not for some ego reason, but because I assumed he must need the water as badly as I needed it for this last leg. It was his water, and I didn't want to deprive him and have the both of us in this decrepit condition! He assured me he would be okay. That he was a professional, experienced, and doing just fine. Finally, I took him up on the water. It seemed like a simple gesture, but one I will never forget! We made it back to Gorak Shep and met the rest of the group.

The next day there was a 360-metre ascent day-climb to Kala Patthar, a location where the summit of Everest is visible. You see, due Everest Base Camp's location in the landscape, you can't see the summit of Everest from there, that's why there was the day trek to Kala Patthar the next morning. However, I chose not to go. I was exhausted. Again, I was managing a careful balancing act with what I could handle at that time. So the answer was pretty obvious to me: I exercised the art of letting go.

17.

IT'S NOT OVER ... YET

Day 10 to Day 13—Descending

Day 10. I joined the rest of the group who did not go to Kala Patthar, and we had breakfast together. And then we started our journey to Pheriche (4,230 m). The others would meet us there later that day.

Have you seen the Nepalese flag before? It's a similar image of the trek we were taking to Pheriche. Uphills, downhills, uphills, downhills. So even though we were heading to a lower altitude, there were still hills to climb. Even still, the walking felt a bit easier for me, I could move faster, and I was able to manage it better. I felt somehow my body had released the tension it had been experiencing over the previous days. I was able to catch up with the group, even when we were going uphill. My energy level seemed to be building too. I felt different. As if the oxygen level in my blood cells had increased. Or my lung capacity had expanded to ease my breathing. Or even some sort of blockages in my inner body had cleared.

I was more chatty on our way back too. As I was more relaxed, I was able to process the conversation and capture what was happening around me on a deeper level.

The team who'd walked to Kala Patthar caught up with us, even though we had an hour head start. Gosh, those guys were fit! It was a bright and sunny day. Such good weather you would hope for while trekking.

After a couple of hours, I could see a village appearing—Pheriche, the village where we would stay the night. That night I acquired some special learning on a subject that I'd yet to consider. Let me share. As you know by now, we'd been staying in different lodges as we trekked. Their dining or common area would have a heater to warm the room. It never crossed my mind to think about the fuel they used for heat.

Driven by curiosity I finally asked the owner of the Pheriche teahouse.

"What do you think?" the owner asked me in return.

"I thought it may be wood, but there aren't many trees that can grow at this altitude".

With a cheeky face, the owner of the teahouse asked, "What do you think is available for us here and is free?"

"Available and free. Hmm …"

I searched through my memory bank. I tried to recall what I'd seen during the trek. At the same time, I was looking around to search for that "thing" that matched the description. Then the universe presented me with a scene right out the window. I could see a yak eating grass from the window where I was sitting. At that moment, my brain seemed to have found the connection. When the group noticed how I fixed my eyes on the yak, some of them burst into laughter.

"Yak dung! There were walls of stacked-up dried yak dung as we passed the villages".

It all made sense.

You may be wondering, "Doesn't it smell?"

I can tell you, "Not at all". A proper drying process does magic.

Day 11. Our destination for the day was a serene village, Kyangjuma, elevation 3,550 metres. The trek took us through several villages until Pangboche, at the base of Ama Dablam. We advanced further and passed through Dingboche and Tengboche, two villages we'd already encountered on our climb up to Everest Base Camp. While we had a brief stop at Tengboche, it reminded me of the night I'd been battling altitude sickness there. It would be a different story that I'd be telling now if I had not pulled through that night. I took a moment to thank this special place, where I'd made it past that special turning point. Thereafter, we went through a steep descent of about 500 metres. We went through rhododendron bushes, and a change in the landscape came into view—fir trees. Another exciting part of trekking, you never know what views are waiting for you.

The steep descent required my ability to shift focus. Although going downhill seems to be easier than going uphill, it represents a different challenge. As you might recall earlier in the book when I talked about descending Mount Kinabalu, it was the added pressure on the knees during that descent, which was noticeably difficult. Simply because the descents from Everest Base Camp, especially this one, tended to be steeper and longer and at such high altitude, the pressure I felt on my knees and the difficulty was pretty big! It takes a careful mental and physical effort because, driven by gravity, your body naturally wants to go faster while descending. You can go faster, but you still need to watch where you place your foot or else you can fall or strain your knees badly to where, say, the next day's descending is too difficult. It took mental focus and strength to slow my body's natural desire to go faster.

After the steep descent—yes, I did it injury-free!—we crossed the bridge over the Dudh Koshi River and passed through a couple of villages, arriving at our destination for the day, Kyangjuma. After setting down our backpacks, we gathered back in the dining area. Gopan arrived about 30 minutes later. What an experienced and sensational trekker! He was able to catch up with us even though we'd had a three-hour head start. Now, why had Gopan not come with us?

Let us rewind the story and go back to the day when I had my altitude sickness. I wasn't the only one who was unwell. Kasey from our team was unwell too. She tried her best to continue on for the next few days. In the end, she made the tough decision to not continue on when we trekked to Gorak Shep and further to Everest Base Camp. She waited and then joined us as we headed down to lower altitudes, but her condition did not improve. Stuart had been keeping Inspired Adventures' (the fundraising agency which organised the entire trip, also mentioned in chapter 11) support team in Sydney informed about Kasey's situation. The support team decided the best way to help her would be to get her to the hospital in Kathmandu. Accordingly, the support team arranged with the in-country team in Nepal to take Kasey by helicopter from Periche to Lukla, and from Lukla by plane to Kathmandu, and to the hospital there.

This morning, Gopan stayed back with Kasey until she was in the good hands of the helicopter team. Then he trekked on his own to meet us at Kyangjuma. Let me add that Kasey recovered and joined us when we were back in Kathmandu.

As I hope you've gathered by now, I consider a person's ability to recognise and then accept the need to discontinue the trek, as Kasey did, and as I'd almost done, a courageous act. Being the person to bring out the stop sign can be very difficult to do. Especially on a trip like this. As you know from my one-year preparation for the trip, all of us participants went through massive efforts to make it to the point where we were in Nepal and trekking. I admired Kasey's decision to withdraw. She'd wanted to do something out of her comfort zone, and she certainly achieved so much by going through the experience. And I was very proud of our superb team as well because everyone showed great respect for Kasey's decision to stop, and to the leaders supporting her in it and ensuring she reached safety.

Day 12. Another long day of trekking, generally downward. We trekked through Namche Bazaar again and decided to take a longer break there. I took the opportunity to walk the town again and sat to enjoy another good look at the surrounding mountain views. I took out my Irish tin whistle and played the traditional Nepali folk song, "Resham Firiri", whose tune I found very catchy when I'd first heard it while researching Nepal. That was when I'd started to learn it. I tried to find the meaning of the song and one particular explanation caught my heart: some people think the song is about a shepherd waiting for his lover from another village to cross the mountain for him. But most say it is a song about chickens and cats without any philosophical and romantic idea behind it. And it is this lack of affectation that makes "Resham Firiri" an ideal folk song. It captures the every-day beauty of Nepali life and details images of love along with traces of humour. It shows the ability of the hill people to laugh even in difficult times. Isn't that wonderful? Oh, I'll add that I had no breathing difficulties when playing this time!

Leaving Namche Bazaar, we continued on downhill to the floor of the river basin and encountered occasional small ascents on our way to the lovely Chumowa village. After dinner, the team had a little pre-celebration. Gopan, Paawan, and Binesh brought us some "Everest Water". They said it was part of a tradition to celebrate the near closing of a trek. If you are wondering, "What is this 'Everest Water'?", it's actually locally-distilled alcohol made from either millet, barley, or rice. The night finished off with music and dancing. We were shown some Nepali dances and discovered that Paawan was quite a dancer himself. The lady owner of the teahouse joined us too. There was also another group heading to Lukla where we too were walking the next day, which made it even merrier. Admittedly, I'm not an overly comfortable dancer, but on that night, I was living it up! Must be the magic of the "Everest Water"!

Day 13. We retraced our steps through the pine forests, past Phakding, where we'd spent the first night of the trek what seemed months earlier but, in fact, was only 12 days earlier. We continued on to Chaunrikhara where we left the main trail to climb the short distance to Lukla, where we'd catch our return flight to Kathmandu the following day.

This day marked both the end of our adventure and my birthday. The whole experience, starting when I'd received that invite email around a year earlier through to the trek itself and the many connections, friendships, and personal discoveries made for the greatest birthday gift.

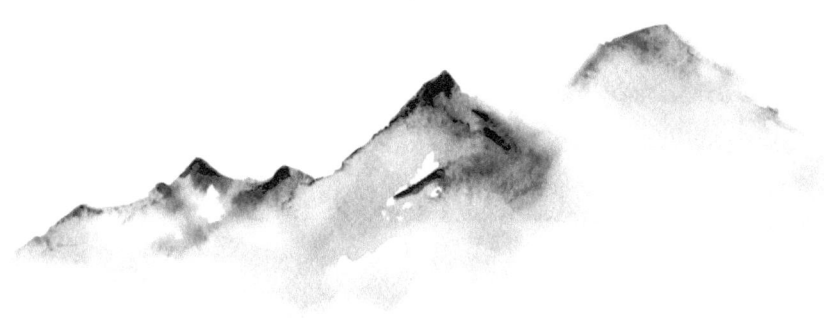

18.

CONCLUSION—SLEEPING DREAMS, WAKE UP!

When I made the decision to embark on this journey, starting with fundraising and training, and then the trekking itself, I expected it would lead me somewhere. However, I wasn't sure what exactly the impact would be. How deeply it would affect me and my life. How enduring it would be.

When, at the end of the trek, Brian, one of the team members, asked me, "Wei, when you return home, what will you do differently?" I found I could easily explain what the impact would be. I didn't have to stop and think of my response. I knew. "I will ask myself to slow down from the busy city life. To be more intentional, more present. I will keep reminding myself not to go through life on auto-pilot. I will continue to look for ways to contribute and serve others in a better way. I know it's not going to be easy, and there will be many times that I'll forget. But I will keep trying".

So how's that been going for me in the 18 months since I completed the trip? I can share with you—the impact persists. When I find myself going through life on auto-pilot mode, the trek reminds me of the importance of living with intention. When I stop thinking of my dreams, the trek brings me back to the vibrancy that living my day-to-day life with a greater purpose allows. When I am afraid of doing something, the trek awakes the hidden courage in me. I suspect, and pray, that the powerful life lessons from this experience will be with me forever.

Five Big Insights

Here are five major takeaways I gained from this experience, insights that I've shared with you already in this book. Let's revisit them together one last time in this final chapter in hopes of reminding ourselves, inspiring ourselves, and giving ourselves that final "yes, I can!" before closing:

- When we have a bigger goal or dream, our life moves from mundane and getting by to vibrant. Electric. Alive!

- Dare to have a dream. Dare to have several dreams. Dare.

- Whether we achieve our dreams depends on how badly we want them. How badly we want them determines how much effort we put into pursuing them. Which results in our achieving them. Or not.

- To achieve our dreams, action is the key. Fear still paralyses me. Fear paralyses all of us. With fear, we can run from it and let it beat us. Or we can stop and look at it straight on. Acknowledge it, acknowledge its presence and the discomfort it brings us, and then act anyway. The more we face fear, the more comfortable we get with the discomfort, which assists us to act anyway. It creates a positive feedback cycle.

- Remember—never aim for perfection. Aim for progression. One step in front of the other. Whether we're on an ascent, a flat, or a descent—one step at a time. That's how we become a better version of ourselves along the journey. Aim to grow!

Time is the only thing no-one can buy. Once it's gone, it's gone. Be courageous! Dare to formulate a dream, and then start acting to reach your dream now. And if you need any encouragement or want to tell me what you are up to, I'd love to hear from you. After all, we're all on this trek together, so the more we can connect and support each other, the more vibrant, grateful, and happy we'll all be.

ACKNOWLEDGMENTS

I've had the privilege of receiving a tremendous amount of support, trust, encouragement, and cheer from so many wonderful people, before, during, and even after returning from Everest Base Camp. From this over-the-top support the inspiration for writing this book was born. Therefore, I would like to take a moment to say a few words of thanks to those who made the journey possible.

Pa, Big Brother, and Second Brother—thank you so much for your encouragement and supporting me in every way as I decided to embark on this journey. You may have been worried at times, but you still chose to stand by me just because it was a dream of mine.

To Jo (Joanna)—thank you so much for looking after me every time I was out training in the bush: "The control tower is always operating for the explorer". And you never failed to answer my questions concerning Australian bush animals and plants.

A huge thank you to everyone in the Big Pot's Squad (as we called our team): Scott, Oliver, Tom, Berlian, Hisela, Clarissa, Karina, Vanessa, Leah, Brody, Gopal, Pemba, and Bilash. You guys are a bunch of phenomenal people who have given me such an extraordinary experience. Even though our time together was short, the moments were priceless.

To my circle of friends, colleagues, friends from my music band, and the teams at Inspired Adventures, Royal Mountain, and UNICEF Australia—I know I have not been able to give all your names, but you are there. I want to give you a shoutout and let you know that you made the difference! Together, we created an amazing journey.

To Nancy, although we have not met in person, I really appreciate your open feedback. Thank you so much for asking me to go deeper into my thoughts as we went through the editing process of this book together. I uncovered many more memory treasures.

This book is written as a way to thank everyone who supported me and who are still supporting me. It is also written for you, my readers. You have reached the end of this book, but I hope it is not the end of your journey. Please take one of the experiences that I have shared and change its details to suit your situation and then go out there to start working on your dream now.

NOW IT'S YOUR TURN
Discover the EXACT 3-step blueprint you need to become a bestselling author in as little as 3 months.

Self-Publishing School helped me, and now I want them to help you with this FREE resource to begin outlining your book!

Even if you're busy, bad at writing, or don't know where to start, you CAN write a bestseller and build your best life.

With tools and experience across a variety of niches and professions, Self-Publishing School is the only resource you need to take your book to the finish line!

Don't Wait.

Say "YES" to becoming a bestseller:

https://self-publishingschool.com/friend/

Follow the steps on the page to get a FREE resource to get started on your book and unlock a discount to get started with Self-Publishing School

ABOUT THE AUTHOR

WEI SAN TANG is an outdoor adventurer, born and raised in Malaysia, and currently living in Sydney. With her parents as outstanding role models of the adventure spirit, she started pushing her limits at an early age and has never stopped. In addition to being an outdoor adventurer, Wei San loves reading books and also playing the flute with her fellow band members. She also enjoys building different structures and objects out of her Nanoblock sets.

Wei San's heartfelt ambition is to spread positivity in our world. She strongly believes a powerful way of doing so is by encouraging others to reach their dreams. She hopes to inspire you through her personal stories.

To learn more about Wei San's adventures and her "mission positivity", and also to tell her about the big dream that you are chasing, connect with her on Facebook @ Tws WeiSan Tang.

CAN YOU HELP?

Thank You for Reading My Book!

I really appreciate all of your feedback,
and I love hearing what you have to say.

I need your input to make the next version
of this book—and my future books—better.

Please leave me an honest review on Amazon,
letting me know what you thought of the book.

Thanks so much!

—Wei San

www.ingramcontent.com/pod-product-compliance
Lightning Source LLC
Chambersburg PA
CBHW021953290426
44108CB00012B/1054